The Answers Are in the Building, Why Top Business Leaders Look Inward to Scale Upward

Copyright © 2026, Jeff Baldassari and Leslie Morales

All rights reserved. No part of this book may be used or reproduced by any means, graphic, electronic, or mechanical, including photocopying, recording, taping or by any information storage retrieval system without the written permission of the author except in the case of brief quotations embodied in critical articles and reviews.

The information presented in The Answers Are in the Building is offered solely for educational and informational purposes, reflecting the authors' perspective on leadership, strategy, and cultural transformation, and it is not intended to serve as a substitute for professional legal, financial, accounting, or specialized business advice. While the authors have exercised due care in preparing this material, they make no warranties or guarantees regarding the specific results or profitability that any individual or business may achieve from applying the principles herein, and the reader should consult qualified professionals for advice tailored to their unique circumstances, with the understanding that the authors assume no liability for the direct or indirect use of this content.

Cover Designer: Edge of Water Designs

Interior Formatting and eBook Design: PublishRight Consulting

ISBNs:

Hardcover 979-8-9886619-4-8

eBook 979-8-9886619-6-2

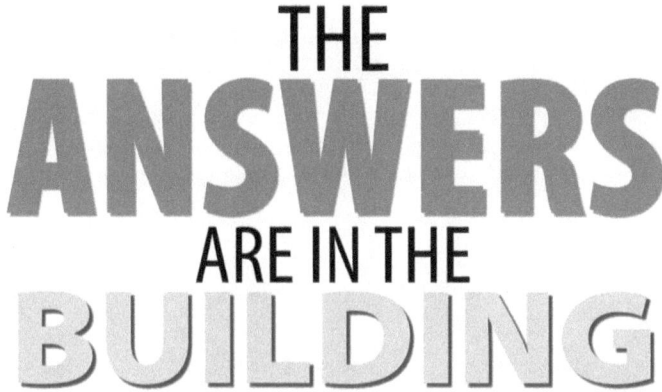

THE ANSWERS ARE IN THE BUILDING

Why Top Business Leaders Look Inward to Scale Upward

JEFF BALDASSARI AND **LESLIE MORALES**

"Once you master navigating the human condition within your organization, you will unleash the answers already in the building and transform your culture."

JEFF BALDASSARI AND LESLIE MORALES

CONTENTS

Notes from the Authors	xiii
Introduction	xv
1. LOOK INWARD TO SCALE UPWARD	1
The Ultimate Leadership Bottleneck: The I-Know-Best Trap	2
Shifting from Problem-Solver to Chief Enabler	3
The Strategic Link: Capacity Through Collaboration	3
The Silent Erosion of Profitability	4
The Promise of Internal Discovery	5
Time to Change	6
The Psychology of Resistance and Buy-In	6
The Necessity of Co-Creation	6
When Things Break Down: The Urgency of Intervention	7
The Inevitable Crisis of Stagnation	7
Unlocking the Golden Nuggets	8
The Solution: Embracing Evolution	8
Action Steps: The Path to Internal Discovery	9
The Imperative: Why Leaders Must Evolve	9
Case Studies: The Proof of Internal Discovery	10
Case Study 1: Manufacturing Turnaround: The Cost of Misdiagnosis	11
Case Study 2: Financial Services Culture Shift: The ROI of Empathy	12
Case Study 3: Crisis Recovery in Logistics: Resilience Through External Perspective	13
The Secret to Successful Scaling: People	15
Diagnosing the Core Issue	16
Unlocking Internal Momentum	16
Action Steps: Mobilizing Your Internal Resources	16
Real-Life Insight: The Power of the Don't Suck! Community	17
Prepare to Scale	18
The Growth Paradox: Building Capacity Before Chasing Sales	19
How to Build the Scalable Foundation	19

Scaling Smart in a Regional E-Commerce Company	20
Case Study 4: The E-Commerce Trap of Uncontrolled Growth	20
Summary	22
2. IT STARTS WITH YOU	**23**
The Mandate of Stabilization	24
Confronting the Full Truth and Isolation	24
The Three Mistakes of the Stabilization Phase	25
Expanding Pillar 1: The Tactics of Modeling	27
The Strategic Mindset: Seeing Opportunity	28
The Foundational Playbook: Three Pillars of Stability	29
The Strategic Imperatives of Proactive Leadership	32
The Cost of Chaos: The Reactive Trap	32
The Strategic Imperative: Capacity as Competitive Advantage	35
Why This Works: Compounding Returns	35
Real-Life Examples: The Proactive Transformation	36
Real-Life Story: Satya Nadella and the Microsoft Turnaround	37
General Motors and the Culture of Proactivity	38
The Leader's Deep Dive – Winning the MVP	39
Summary	40
3. EFFECTIVE LEADERSHIP: THE ENGINE OF SCALE	**43**
The Crisis of Top-Down Control	44
The Pitfalls of Command and Compliance	44
The Strategic Blindness to the Why	45
Leaders Who Inspire: The Shift to Co-Creation	46
From Prescription to Co-Creation	46
The Leader on the Sidelines: Trading Intervention for Influence	47
The Heartbeat of Authentic Dialogue	48
The ROI of Empowerment: Action and Returns	49
Operationalizing Collaboration	49
The Tangible Returns of Collaborative Leadership	50
Supportive Leadership: The Protective Filter	52
The Shift from Reactive to Anticipatory	53
The Protective Filter: Protection Over Delegation	53
The Courage of Accountability	54
Action and Returns of Supportive Leadership	55
The Discipline of Supportive Leadership	55

    Case Studies   56
        Satya Nadella at Microsoft: The Culture Catalyst   57
        Buffer: The Protective Filter in Action   60
    Summary: Leadership as the Engine of Sustainable Growth   60

4. CREATING RESULTS TOGETHER: THE COLLABORATIVE ENGINE OF GROWTH   63
    The Strategic Power of Problems   63
    The Discipline of Root Cause Analysis   64
    Cross-Department Problem Solving   68
    New Results Require New Ideas: Embracing Proactive Evolution   71
    Creating Opportunity From Failure   74
    Case Study: BrightPath Solutions   77
    Summary: Sustainable Solutions Through Collaborative Internal Inquiry   79

5. RESIST SCALING FROM THE OUTSIDE   81
    The Gold Standard of Growth: Inward Focus, Outward Impact   82
    The Traps of External Validation   84
    Building from the Inside Out   85
    From Theory to Internal Strength   86
        Pinpoint Your Target   86
        Commit to Customization   86
        Validate from Within   87
        Build Trust Capital   87
    The Enduring Value of Internal Focus   88
    Case Study: CustomTech Solutions – The Power of the Inside Game   89
    Summary: Resisting FOMO and Scaling from the Inside Out   91

6. FOSTERING A POSITIVE CULTURE   93
    The Cultural Blueprint: From Architect to Gardener   94
        Policies: The Silent Architects of Culture   95
    A Trusting Environment: The Antidote to Toxicity   96
        The Tug-of-War: Control vs. Contribution   96
        Conflict as a Catalyst for Growth   97
    The Leader's Toolkit: Cultivating Solutions   98
        1. Model Vulnerability and Authenticity   98
        2. Empower Decision-Making at All Levels   99
        3. Create Safe Spaces for Honest Conversation   99

    4. Recognize and Celebrate Contributions   99
    5. Embrace and Leverage Differences   100
  Case Study: Cultural Repair in Action   100
  A Balanced Environment: The Key to Sustainable Excellence   101
    The Vicious Cycle of Control and Burnout   101
    The Path to Sustainable Influence   102
    The Mandate for Sustainable Culture   103
    Case Study: Harmony Foods   104
  Summary: The Answers Are in the Culture   105

7. INCREASING EMPLOYEE ENGAGEMENT   107
  The True Cost of Engagement: Why Teams Trump Solo Acts   107
    The Disengagement Crisis and The Financial Imperative   107
    The Hidden Iceberg: Intangible Costs of Disengagement   108
    The Problem with Paying for Partial Success   109
    Beyond the Paycheck: The Power of Contribution   112
  Leading Change with Purpose: The Power of Internal Narrative   113
    Data Drives Decisions, Stories Drive People   113
  Four Disciplines for Purposeful Change   114
    1. Launch with Narrative: Communicate Change with Purpose and Story   114
    2. Activate the Inner Circle: Engage Key Employees Early for Buy-In   114
    3. Campaign for Change: Practice Internal Marketing   114
    4. Foster Collective Ownership: Create Opportunities for Contribution   115
  The Foundation of Trust and Accountability   115
    Trust: The Single Biggest Accelerator   115
    The Low Engagement Trap and Psychological Safety   116
    The Power of Appreciative Inquiry: Shifting from Deficit to Design   117
  The Leader's Mandate: The Accountability Accelerator   120
  Recognition and Growth: The Compounding Value of Investment   121
    The Power of Proactive Recognition   121
    Investing in Growth and Capability: The ROI Case   121
    Promoting for Success: The Dual Career Track Model   122

Case Studies: Principles in Practice	124
Case Study A: Summit Financial Group (Trust and Contribution)	124
Case Study B: Horizon Health Systems (Proactive Investment)	126
Summary: The Full Engagement Framework	129
Final Action Checklist: The Engagement Blueprint	130
8. YOUR SECRET GROWTH DRIVER: SECOND CHANCE EMPLOYMENT	**131**
Walk the Talk—Confronting the Leadership Barrier	132
Unmasking Leadership Bias: The Subtlety of Sabotage	132
Creating Awareness and Systemic Mitigation	134
The Economics of Opportunity—Calculating the ROI	136
The Hidden Cost of Churn	136
The Loyalty Dividend and Discretionary Effort	136
Strategic Integration—Talent Pipeline by Design	137
Mapping the Program to Capacity Needs	137
Leveraging External Ecosystems	138
The Cultural Force Multiplier	139
Redefining Corporate Values in Action	139
The Power of Empathy and Perspective	139
Debunking the Myths—Addressing Common Concerns	140
Safety Concerns and Perceived Risk	140
Managing Cultural Resistance and Integration	141
The Implementation System—Solutions and Action Steps	142
The Five-Step Implementation System: How to Execute	142
Support Systems: Investing in Retention	144
Case Study: Fresh Start Logistics	144
Summary: The Strategic Imperative of Second-Chance Inclusion	146
Epilogue: The Architect Within	**149**
About the Authors	**153**

NOTES FROM THE AUTHORS

The strategies and lessons in this book were forged in the trenches of business. They represent the accumulation of three decades of real-world experience built from the successes, the failures, and the simple, profound truth that we've witnessed time and again.

For me, Jeff, that journey includes two decades as a President & CEO for two manufacturers, serving on seven boards, and founding The Competitive Edge Group in 2024. Throughout my career, whether advising ambitious founders or experienced CEOs of multi-million-dollar corporations, one fundamental truth has proven itself: the answers to scaling a business aren't found in a textbook, a new technology, or a high-priced, outside consultant.

For me, Leslie, the insights were drawn from over three decades of building businesses from the ground up across various industries, including hospitality, service, automotive, and manufacturing. I learned invaluable lessons by making mistakes, working through them, and enlisting the advice and contributions of employees at all levels.

Together, we've found that the key to success lies within every organization, but to uncover the key, you must first ask diverse groups of your employees the right questions. The answers are in the building, your building. They reside within the minds and hearts of your people, and in the institutional knowledge you've built over time.

Jeff Baldassari and Leslie Morales
January 2026

INTRODUCTION

This book is a roadmap to a different kind of business leadership—one rooted in experience, not academic theory. It is an urgent call to action for every leader who knows, deep down, that their organization is capable of more. We wrote this book because we believe that when seeking the most profound transformation a business can undergo, leaders must not look outside their walls, but within them.

For too long, leaders have chased the fantasy that exponential growth will magically fix internal problems. We are here to challenge that fantasy. Growth does not fix flaws. It exposes them and amplifies them. It turns small cracks in your operational foundation into gaping holes. If your operational house is not in order, the sheer weight of rapid growth will bring it crashing down.

That is why we believe with every fiber of our being that operational excellence must precede lead generation. You must first get your house in order. This book will guide you through the critical, often overlooked steps required to streamline your processes, build a resilient team, and transform your business culture from the inside out.

The message of this book is simple: The answers are in the build-

INTRODUCTION

ing. They reside within the minds and hearts of your people, and in the institutional knowledge you built over time. Yet, leaders often fall into the trap of believing they must have all the answers. This destructive mindset leads to predictable outcomes: micromanagement, an unhealthy reliance on those who agree with everything a leader says and the stifling of both fresh perspectives and genuine contribution.

This book is not about giving up control. It is about shifting from merely managing people to inspiring and influencing them. This is how you build a business culture where employees feel a genuine sense of ownership in their company and have trust in their management, allowing the business to weather any storm. In these pages, you will discover a proven process to unlock the wisdom and potential that already exists within your organization.

The Chasm Between Business 101 and Mastery

Much of this book's content will be recognizable from Business 101. And, indeed, the framework is elegantly simple with concepts so straightforward you could write them out on a napkin.

However, here is where that elegant theory slams into a brick wall. A business, or any organization, is a result of complex human interactions, something most business leaders fail to realize. They fail to realize this, not because they lack intelligence or strategy, but because they lack the core human skills needed for internal alignment. They are often wedded to top-down management—the mindset that screams: "I'm the boss, the founder, the person with the big title, and everyone has to do as I say because I know best!"

A leader with this traditional, ego-driven approach—the I-know-best syndrome—stifles innovation and trust as they are often lacking in empathy, lacking the ability to read a room, and lacking the capacity to seek contributions from all levels of employees. All this means is they are unable to build rapport with their workforce.

This book is not about simple business concepts. It is about the

INTRODUCTION

deft hand needed to manage the culture and people within your business. The true complexity lies in managing the people part of the equation. For example,

Navigating Organizational Silos and Turf Wars

- **The Challenge.** How do you get department heads (who are accustomed to protecting their own budget and resources) to celebrate a success that originated in another division?
- **The Barrier.** Office politics and vested interests often hamper the simplest of tasks. Few department heads like to share credit or cede control of their project to another department head.

Overcoming Complacency and the Why-Change Mentality

- **The Challenge.** How do you motivate high-performing but risk-averse teams (or individuals) to change a profitable status quo, even one that is unsustainable?
- **The Barrier.** Complacency breeds inertia. The effort required for true Appreciative Inquiry is high and without a skilled guide, teams will prioritize short-term comfort over the long-term, aspirational benefits of transformation.

Managing the Hippo Effect (Highest Paid Person's Opinion)

- **The Challenge.** How do you ensure that the insights and ideas of entry-level employees or front-line staff are given consideration and weighed equally against the ideas of more senior employees and, in addition, are not overridden

by the presence of the senior executive or the founder in the room?
- **The Barrier.** The power dynamic in most organizations can be daunting to experience. The gravitational pull of the title or the largest salary can shut down genuine dialogue, even when a leader *thinks* they are encouraging contribution. The deft hand is needed to counter this bias and ensure all voices carry equal weight.

We have learned these difficult lessons in the trenches of business. We manage the people part of the equation by providing the necessary deft hand so our clients can remain laser-focused on business opportunities and realize the full potential of the proven process.

Your Greatest Asset and the Untapped Resource

Your employees are your most valuable asset. The leadership framework shown in this book emphasizes transforming your approach by ensuring your people feel valued, seen, and heard.

We encourage you not to rely on traditional, top-down methodologies and embrace new ideas from every corner of your organization, and even from your entry-level employees.

This commitment to relying on your people extends to untapped talent pools. We strongly encourage you to explore the vast potential of returning citizens who were formerly incarcerated. These individuals often bring extraordinary focus, loyalty, and determination to the workplace.

Offering opportunities to this population is not only a moral imperative but also a powerful source of talent that can bolster your workforce and contribute to a resilient culture.

By changing your perspective and implementing the roadmap

INTRODUCTION

found in these pages, you will unlock the full potential of your workforce and position your business for resilient, sustainable growth.

The most profound insights are not always the most complicated. They are often the most fundamental. Your journey to scaling your business starts right here, with a simple, profound truth: the answers are in the building. Let's find them together.

CHAPTER 1
LOOK INWARD TO SCALE UPWARD

Success can be a double-edged sword. When a business is thriving, hitting sales targets and riding a wave of revenue, the instinct is to chase more sales, more customers, and faster growth. This outward pursuit of momentum is intoxicating, yet it often hides a critical truth. Beneath the surface of that success, inefficiencies and systemic dysfunctions often lurk, quietly draining profits and eroding long-term sustainability. These hidden problems don't magically vanish; they simply get buried under the noise of increased revenue.

We've seen this pattern play out repeatedly. High-growth companies that appear strong are unknowingly bleeding cash through internal missteps. The urgency to scale outward blinds leaders to the all-important need to first look inward. And that, precisely, is where the greatest opportunity for resilient, sustainable growth lies.

The costliest mistake a leader can make is operating under the delusion that growth will fix everything. Here is the reality: growth amplifies what is already broken. If your business is struggling with erratic cash flow, shrinking margins, or persistent operational headaches, the cause is rarely the market or the competition. Indeed, it's almost always a lack of discipline and accountability within your own walls.

The Ultimate Leadership Bottleneck: The I-Know-Best Trap

Why do otherwise intelligent leaders consistently fail to see the answers within their own walls? The cause is frequently a pervasive leadership dysfunction: the **I-Know-Best Trap.**

This mindset is not born from malice, but from initial success as, say, when the founder or the CEO who successfully navigated the company's early, chaotic stages develops a protective but ultimately destructive belief that their experience trumps all.

This mindset creates the ultimate organizational bottleneck. It fosters a culture of dependence where employees are rewarded for compliance rather than contribution, and their primary function is to execute decisions from on high, and not to offer innovative ideas.

When a leader operates from this pedestal, they unwittingly signal to their team that their voice is simply a tool, not a source of valuable insight. This lack of genuine curiosity and the inability to build rapport with the workforce can swiftly become active liabilities.

When leaders stop truly listening, they lose the ability to read the room; and they fail to seek contribution because they are already convinced they possess the superior solution. The result? Valuable insights remain buried, hidden behind an invisible wall of top-down authority. The leader remains the single limiting factor in the company's ability to evolve.

Shifting from Problem-Solver to Chief Enabler

To escape the **I-Know-Best Trap** and truly unlock the wisdom of your team, a fundamental shift in the leader's operational identity must occur. That is, you must move from being the Chief Problem-Solver to the Chief Enabler.

The Chief Problem-Solver focuses on symptoms. They spend their days jumping from fire to fire, making critical decisions in a vacuum and constantly reinforcing the notion that the organization cannot function without their direct intervention. This creates brilliant firefighters but terrible owners of process.

The Chief Enabler, by contrast, focuses on systems. Their primary job is to design the environment where the answers to those persistent fires—can be found by the people closest to the work. This transition requires a conscious effort to build empathy and trust. It demands a leader who is comfortable admitting they don't have all the answers and who is willing to delegate not just the task, but the intellectual ownership of the solution.

This shift is not about giving up control. It is about gaining leverage. When you empower your team to solve systemic issues, you gain back countless hours previously spent on operational firefighting, and you convert compliance into emotional ownership, making your employees the proactive champions of change rather than the passive recipients of new mandates. This is the only way to build a resilient, self-correcting organization that can sustain growth beyond the influence of a single leader.

The Strategic Link: Capacity Through Collaboration

The necessity of **Capacity First, Growth Second**, the central tenet for scalable operations, is inextricably linked to internal discovery and co-creation. You cannot accurately audit your operational capacity if your audit process is top-down and blind to the realities on the ground of your business.

Capacity assessment is not just a calculation on a spreadsheet; it is an act of collaboration. Your employees, particularly those on the front line, have the most accurate, granular data on where friction occurs, where time is wasted, and what processes are redundant. Their daily experience *is* your capacity data.

For example, when an AI (Appreciative Inquiry) session structures conversations around "What if?" (Dream Phase), the team collaboratively envisions what could be achieved if current systems were scalable. The subsequent "So what?" (Design Phase) forces them to identify the structural and systemic investments necessary to support that vision. This directly translates into an honest, internal capacity review guided by the very people who perform the work.

This approach transforms the often-dreaded capacity review from a bureaucratic exercise into a collective strategic endeavor. It ensures that when you do resume scaling, the investments—whether in training, automation, or staffing—are targeted, validated, and immediately supported by the people who designed them.

Discipline creates predictable growth because a disciplined, empowered team is an accurate, scalable team. By making internal discovery a continuous practice, you ensure that your capacity is always growing just ahead of your sales, turning a potential chaos point into your ultimate competitive advantage.

The Silent Erosion of Profitability

These internal issues are not always dramatic failures. They are often silent, consistent erosions of capital. Consider the money that leaders are likely leaving on the table right now through:

- **Unmanaged Receivables:** Lack of oversight effectively transforms valuable working capital into interest-fee loans to the customers who pay late.
- **Missed Discounts:** ignoring small vendor discounts or failing to verify service charges due to procedural slack.
- **Flawed Incentives:** using compensation systems that reward activity instead of outcomes, driving up costs without delivering true value.
- **Operational Drag:** tolerating (i) excessive material handling, (ii) redundant process steps, and (iii) poor inventory management are silent killers that chip away at every percentage point of profitability.

This constant internal leakage, this hidden tax on your success, is often simply accepted as the cost of doing business. It is not. It is the cost of unwillingness to confront the shortcomings of your business operations.

The Promise of Internal Discovery

The good news is that these problems are entirely fixable. The solutions do not require luck, external market shifts, or a massive injection of outside capital. They require discipline, accountability, and a willingness to confront your operational processes, even if doing so makes you uncomfortable. We've made it our mission to help organizations uncover the hidden value they already possess. The fundamental truth remains: the answers are almost always already in the building.

This book is your guide to that discovery process. It's the methodology that will teach you how to shift your focus from frustrating external problems to exciting internal possibilities. If you're ready to find the $100,000—or significantly more—hiding within your business, it starts here, by taking a courageous look inward.

Time to Change

To truly scale upward, you must first commit to change. Not just surface-level adjustments, but a deep, introspective shift in how your entire organization operates and, crucially, how your people engage with its core mission. Exploring the mindset and urgency required to begin this transformation is the key to facilitating change that sticks.

The Psychology of Resistance and Buy-In

It is often said that people don't like change. That is not true. What they resist is change that feels arbitrary, top-down, or disconnected from their reality. When change is purposefully designed to eliminate daily frustrations and deliver real, meaningful results, people lean in. They engage. They champion the new way because they helped design it.

The most effective transformations begin by actively engaging the front line worker. When leadership takes the time to sit with employees, ask thoughtful, challenging questions, and truly listen, trust is built, and executable ideas begin to flow. Strategizing based solely on hierarchy is short-sighted. When leaders welcome ideas and solutions from every corner of their organization, they create emotional ownership. The outcome is that your people will not just comply with change; they will champion it.

The Necessity of Co-Creation

Commitment to listening forms the foundation of a co-creative partnership. The best clients are not chasing volume; they are pursuing organizational alignment. They are coachable, open to being challenged, and understand that clinging to, "but this is the way we've always done it" is a fast track to stagnation and irrelevance. Together, we co-create solutions, challenge assumptions, and achieve outcomes that are not only impactful but deeply sustainable. Why? Because the team helped build them.

When Things Break Down: The Urgency of Intervention

The need for change becomes acute when operational effectiveness has simply stopped functioning. Leadership gets stuck in analysis paralysis, constantly asking, "How do we get out of this mess?" The old playbook no longer applies.

A fractional engagement—bringing in an experienced, objective peer—can be transformative. This intervention allows existing leaders to grow by learning directly from someone who has successfully navigated similar challenges, pulling the organization out of the echo chamber where bad ideas simply recycle themselves. Until leadership makes the courageous decision to invite outside professionals to guide these deep, introspective engagements, they remain trapped in a cycle of, as the saying goes, not knowing what they don't know. Change isn't just necessary to capture hidden value. It's urgent to stop the bleeding.

The Inevitable Crisis of Stagnation

What happens when a business ignores the quiet erosion of its profits? Operations no longer function well. Leadership finds itself at a loss because the playbooks that delivered success yesterday inhibit growth today. This is the crisis of stagnation in which old methods become costly liabilities.

We often encounter leaders trapped in a cycle of confusion that is fueled by their fear that people do not like change. This fear prevents evolution. The truth is, clinging to the way things have always been done is a recipe for stagnation at best, and a guarantee of decline at worst. To break this cycle, leadership must recognize that the failure is not external, it is internal and it is procedural and cultural. The answer is not to search for a new market trend, but to challenge assumptions and transform culture to achieve sustainable outcomes.

Unlocking the Golden Nuggets

When leadership shifts its mindset from avoiding discomfort to pursuing breakthroughs, the organization discovers its own **Golden Nuggets,** the hidden value that was always in the building.

The first nugget is realizing that change can be good when it is meant to produce results. This requires a courageous commitment to challenging assumptions. Leaders must question every procedure, every departmental silo, and every long-held belief about how things are done.

The ultimate golden nugget lies in cultural transformation. When you invite your teams to co-create the solutions—the new SOPs, the more effective workflow—they develop emotional ownership. This commitment turns internal problems into co-created solutions, proving that the most powerful, immediate sources of capital and efficiency are found by looking inward.

The Solution: Embracing Evolution

The moment a leader accepts that internal processes need to evolve because they've become stale, the solution presents itself. What worked effectively when the company was half its size is now the bottleneck that limits future growth. Tolerating the status quo is the riskiest decision you will ever make.

The solution requires a fundamental commitment to strategic evolution. By framing change as a disciplined, collaborative endeavor —not a panicked reaction—a leader transforms their role from enforcer of static rules to curator of dynamic growth. This commitment to constant self-assessment and adaptation is the ultimate competitive advantage. A genuinely adaptive culture cannot be easily copied.

Action Steps: The Path to Internal Discovery

The transformation process begins with structured actions designed to expose hidden inefficiencies and harness latent potential. To do this you must:

1. **Audit and Assess Current Operations.** You cannot fix what you don't understand. Conduct a thorough, data-driven review of existing processes to identify inefficiencies and bottlenecks. We focus heavily on process mapping—visualizing every step of the customer journey to pinpoint where unnecessary friction occurs.
2. **Initiate a Change Management Program.** Once pain points are identified, introduce change purposefully. Develop a structured plan that includes clear communication, targeted training, and robust support systems. The new processes are presented as solutions co-developed with employee input, thus mitigating resistance.
3. **Foster a Culture of Innovation and Adaptability.** The goal is to create an organization that is inherently self-correcting. Encourage open dialogue, experimentation, and continuous learning to shift the mindset from resistance to acceptance of change. Leaders must model curiosity and reward small-scale, thoughtful experimentation to reduce employee fears of making mistakes.

The Imperative: Why Leaders Must Evolve

The decision to look inward and commit to change is an act of competitive survival. Stagnation threatens growth far more than any market downturn might. When a company becomes comfortable with its existing procedures, it risks falling behind competitors and losing relevance.

This urgency exists because yesterday's solutions cannot solve today's problems. The successful playbook from five years ago is likely a cumbersome liability today. If a process requires manual handoffs that software could automate, the company is effectively choosing to pay its employees to perform repetitive, low-value work. The only way forward is to embrace the uncomfortable truth that continuous evolution is the only constant. This commitment to internal assessment is how cultural transformation drives sustainability. The time has come to stop managing the friction and start building the future.

Case Studies: The Proof of Internal Discovery

When a mid-sized manufacturer nearly collapsed under the weight of late deliveries, and when a financial services firm suffered a crippling turnover crisis, both leadership teams sought expensive solutions such as analyzing the competition and the markets and buying high-tech software. Similarly, when a logistics company faced a catastrophic system breakdown, they were paralyzed by internal blame, unable to diagnose their own process failures.

Yet, in all three cases, whether the answer was a simple floor-plan redesign, a new recognition program, or the intervention of an objective peer, the most valuable and enduring solutions were not found in acquisitions or costly new resources. They were discovered by deliberately turning our focus inward, listening to the wisdom of the existing workforce, and applying objective expertise to the internal environment.

This book is founded on the principle that your organization's ultimate potential is not a prize to be won outside your walls, but a resource waiting to be unlocked inside your building.

Case Study 1: Manufacturing Turnaround: The Cost of Misdiagnosis

A regional, mid-sized manufacturer of specialized components—a company built on a 40-year legacy—was not just struggling; it was facing a survival crisis. For the previous eighteen months, the business had been steadily bleeding cash at an alarming rate, driven by a cycle of late deliveries and skyrocketing operational costs.

The company's leadership team, headquartered in a newly renovated administrative wing, was convinced the problem was external. Their strategy sessions were dominated by discussions about market volatility, the unreliability of foreign suppliers, and labor shortages. They were actively vetting expensive solutions like implementing new enterprise resource planning (ERP) software and even considering moving production overseas—all costly, risky measures, and all based on the assumption that the answer lay *outside* the building.

The morale on the factory floor was predictably low. The frontline warehouse staff (the people responsible for the physical flow of every single product) felt the pressure acutely, spending their days rushing to meet deadlines only to be tripped up by their operating system.

Instead of searching outside for complex, expensive fixes, their team took the premise of this book to heart, and looked inward. It did not start with a high-tech audit; it started with a pair of steel-toed boots and a conversation. Engaging directly with the frontline warehouse staff immediately illuminated the true, internal culprit: excessive, non-value-added handling of goods caused by an outdated, labyrinthine floor layout. The parts were being moved and touched up to five times before ever hitting the shipping dock, creating a massive, invisible operational drag, albeit not invisible to the warehouse workers..

By establishing a co-creation initiative—empowering and involving the staff to redesign their own floor plan using visual and lean manufacturing principles—they completely streamlined the process. This shift resulted in a 40% reduction in the material handling time of goods and parts, which eliminated the backlog, restored reliable delivery schedules, and generated savings of over $250,000 annually.

The Takeaway. This case proved that the solution was not a half-million-dollar software package or a high-risk relocation; it was a simple, elegant realization. The most valuable, immediate, and high-impact capital was hidden in the untapped ingenuity and efficiency of their existing operations and the people who knew the process best.

Case Study 2: Financial Services Culture Shift: The ROI of Empathy

The financial services sector thrives on stability and expertise, but this regional firm was teetering on the edge of a human capital crisis. They were experiencing a crippling combination of high employee turnover, especially among their top-performing analysts and widespread, noticeable low morale. This brain drain was severely impacting client relationships, slowing project completion, and forcing managers to divert crucial time toward constant and expensive recruiting.

In response, the executive leadership team defaulted to the most obvious and expensive solution: compensation. They initiated market adjustments, offering modest salary bumps and year-end bonuses, convinced that their best talent was simply being poached by competitors offering more money. The budget was strained, but the core problems persisted, leaving the leadership puzzled and frustrated. They believed they were investing heavily in their people, yet the talent still walked out the door.

The executive suite's blind spot was believing that transactional rewards (money) were the ultimate motivators, while ignoring the relational and psychological needs of their workforce. To uncover the answers, leadership moved past the spreadsheets and held confidential listening sessions with employees at all levels, from new hires to mid-level managers. The root cause was not a dollar amount. It was a deep, pervasive sense of being invisible. Staff felt their hard work was taken for granted due to a complete lack of genuine, meaningful recognition. Crucially, they lacked clear, transparent career paths, leading to the belief that promotion was based on subjective favor rather than measurable achievement.

The solution was two-fold, remarkably inexpensive, and entirely internal:

1. **Transparency & Trust.** The firm introduced structured, transparent promotion criteria for every role, clearly mapping out the skills and metrics required for advancement. This instantly quelled anxiety and resentment fueled by uncertainty.
2. **Genuine Recognition.** Leadership created a peer-nominated recognition program that celebrated not just results, but effort, collaboration, and demonstration of company values.

Within nine months, the firm achieved a massive 30% improvement in employee retention, saving hundreds of thousands in recruitment and training costs. Productivity rose significantly because employees were finally clear on their path forward and felt genuinely valued.

The Takeaway. This firm discovered that sustainable profit is not merely a function of financial transactions but a direct result of tending to the fundamental human side of business—cultivating trust, providing clarity, and offering authentic recognition. The ultimate driver of success was already present in their people; it just needed to be seen and validated.

Case Study 3: Crisis Recovery in Logistics: Resilience Through External Perspective

This regional logistics company specialized in high-volume, just-in-time delivery for dozens of businesses across the state. They understood efficiency, but their internal structure was fragile. The crisis hit immediately after the launch of a major, months-in-the-making system upgrade. What was intended to be a leap forward in efficiency instantly became a catastrophic operational breakdown.

In the following weeks, the organization descended into chaos: thousands of orders were lost or mismatched, customer complaints surged to unprecedented levels, and the reputation built over a decade began to erode. Internally, the leadership dissolved into a state of fear and rampant finger-pointing. The IT team blamed Operations for insufficient testing; Operations blamed IT for a flawed rollout; and the CEO blamed the expensive external consulting firm that managed the upgrade.

This failure wasn't just technical; it was a crisis of internal objectivity. The leaders were too deeply entangled in the disaster—and too busy defending their own departments—to see a clear path out. They were trapped in the classic cycle of not knowing what they do not know, unable to diagnose the root systemic and cultural failures that allowed the software to fail so completely.

The Solution: Inviting an Objective Professional

Recognizing the gravity of the situation, the board made the crucial decision to seek external objectivity, bringing in a fractional executive —a high-level, temporary professional with no personal stake in the internal blame game.

This peer intervention allowed for:

1. **Immediate Stabilization.** This occurred when the executive quickly moved to isolate the core technical failure and restore rudimentary order, stemming the financial and customer bleed.
2. **Cross-Functional Reconstruction.** This occurred when they bypassed the fragmented departmental leadership and established a cross-functional task force charged not just with fixing the system, but with rebuilding the failed processes and the broken trust.

The company's recovery was remarkable. They not only returned to pre-breakdown stability but emerged significantly stronger and more resilient. They instituted genuinely collaborative processes, built strong communication bridges across departments, and developed a newly transparent, highly collaborative culture.

The Takeaway. This firm demonstrated that when internal leadership is too close to a crisis, bringing in objective, external professionals is not an expense, it is an urgent requirement needed to make the necessary changes. Unless leadership invites this outside perspective to guide the engagement, they will remain trapped in the cycle of their own blind spots. Change is often terrifying, but when faced head-on, it becomes the catalyst for everything that follows.

The Secret to Successful Scaling: People

We have established the financial and operational urgency to look inward. Now, we reveal where the most powerful and scalable solution lies: within your people. Systems and strategies are only ideas until your team brings them to life. If your company feels stuck, the root cause is rarely the market. It's that way because your talent is not engaged, empowered and aligned.

The cornerstone truth of this book: the answers are in your building. Your team holds a wealth of knowledge, tactical insight, and untapped potential. They see the operational friction points that leadership often can't. But those invaluable ideas only surface in the right environment—one where people feel heard, valued, and trusted. Scaling successfully is about unlocking the full potential of the people you already have. It's time to collaborate inward with the ultimate growth engine: your team.

Diagnosing the Core Issue

Stalled revenues, inefficient operations, and a dysfunctional culture are nearly always symptoms of a single issue: your people are not fully engaged or empowered in the solution process. Thinking the solutions must come from outside sources ignores the immense, untapped intellectual capital already sitting on your payroll. The secret to success is, and always has been, people.

Unlocking Internal Momentum

Getting unstuck comes down to one key concept: using the people in your organization. This requires a disciplined shift in leadership focus. As leaders, our primary job is not to have all the answers. It is to create an environment where the answers can be found.

First, surround yourself with supportive and talented people. This is the most immediate action you can take. Second, shift from being the chief problem solver to the chief enabler. This process of deep internal engagement is the only way to transform a stagnating business into a resilient, adaptive, and high-growth enterprise.

Action Steps: Mobilizing Your Internal Resources

The shift from stagnation to exponential growth is achieved through action and commitment to internal mobilization.

1. **Empower Your Team to Solve Problems.** Stop looking outside for answers. Host regular, structured cross-functional meetings or listening sessions designed explicitly to surface insights and co-create solutions to systemic problems.
2. **Build Momentum Through Focused Execution.** Momentum doesn't come from half-measures. It comes from consistent, intentional action. Set short-term goals

that are achievable and visible, then vigorously celebrate progress. Use those small, visible wins to reinforce a culture of movement and accountability.
3. **Surround Yourself with Supportive and Talented People.** Your success is directly tied to the quality and alignment of your team. Objectively evaluate your current team dynamics and invest strategically in coaching, development, or strategic hiring to strengthen your internal community.

Real-Life Insight: The Power of the Don't Suck! Community

Even outside the cold, high-stakes environment of the boardroom or the factory floor, the principle that success depends on leveraging the talent and cohesion of your people holds true. Consider my (Jeff's) local pool-league team, the delightfully named Don't Suck!

For years, we have been unlikely champions, consistently outperforming teams with greater individual skills. While our individual talents vary widely, we've brought home more than a half dozen championship trophies in less than two years. How? It is not because of our abilities, but because of how we operate.

Our success is built on a few simple, non-negotiable cultural rules:

1. **Relentless Support.** No one is left alone after a bad shot. We surround the struggling player with encouragement, focus their strategy for the next rack, and never tolerate blame or frustration.
2. **Communication with Purpose.** Before every crucial game, we discuss strategy, not just shots. We align on who is playing which opponent and identify the strengths and weaknesses of the other team. We are a single, coordinated unit.
3. **Shared Accountability.** Every player is responsible for contributing, and the team success is owned equally. When we win, we all win. When we lose, we learn together.

This dynamic applies directly to your business operations. When you surround yourself with the right people—the ones you already have—and you deliberately foster a genuine culture of collaboration, support, and shared accountability, you build a team that wins consistently, no matter the skill of the competition.

The real secret to scaling, to achieving that exponential growth your company deserves, isn't found in a complicated spreadsheet, a new piece of software, or an expensive external merger. It's found in the collective wisdom, motivation, and beliefs of your people. Stop looking outside for the magic bullet. Start looking inward. Your championship is already in the building.

Prepare to Scale

Scaling isn't a chaotic scramble; it's a disciplined and intentional strengthening of what is already working. After recognizing the power of your people, the next critical step is to prepare your entire organization to grow from the inside out. **This demands a fundamental mindset shift: true growth isn't just about sales. It's about capacity.**

Many businesses make the fatal mistake of launching aggressive growth plans without first evaluating whether their internal systems can support this growth. The result? Bottlenecks in production, fulfillment, and customer service. True scaling begins with discipline. The most successful companies do not just sell more, they build more capacity.

One powerful tool to guide this preparation is Appreciative Inquiry (AI). This framework helps teams collaboratively envision and act on their core strengths by structuring conversations around:

- **What if?** (Dream). What could we achieve if we scaled the very best parts of our current operation?

- **So what?** (Design). What is the measurable impact of this vision, and what core systems must be in place to support it?
- **Now what?** (Design). What small, intentional actions will we take this week to bring that future into our present capacity?

Now answer, "Are you confident your organization can grow without imploding?" If the answer is not a resounding "yes," it is time to get your house in order—before you scale.

The Growth Paradox: Building Capacity Before Chasing Sales

The most vital Golden Nugget is that the first step to growth and scaling is not sales; it's capacity. Doubling down on what your company does best is far more profitable than chasing the latest trend.

The main problem arises because companies fail to analyze their departmental capacities before they launch a new growth plan. If your operational leaders do not know each department's capacity at all times, a systemic failure is inevitable.

The solution is to commit to discipline over distraction. This requires a clear focus on execution. To achieve sustainable growth, leaders must anticipate where they will need to expand and then invest in those areas before you're forced to do so.

How to Build the Scalable Foundation

The shift from a reactive scramble to predictable growth requires a disciplined application of the look inward philosophy.

- **Capacity First, Growth Second.** Conduct a rigorous capacity review across operations, fulfillment, customer service, and leadership to identify potential bottlenecks.

Scaling without capacity leads to chaos. Internal readiness is the foundation of sustainable success.
- **Scaling Through Shared Strengths.** Facilitate a team session using the "**What if? So what? Now what?**" framework to spark engagement. Your strengths are your launchpad. It helps you scale by building on what's already working.
- **Discipline Over Distraction.** Reinforce daily operational discipline by setting clear priorities and eliminating distractions.
- **Discipline Creates Predictable Growth.** While others chase trends, disciplined companies build infrastructure, refine processes, and grow steadily.

Scaling Smart in a Regional E-Commerce Company

This is an excellent final case study that directly addresses the concept of **sustainable growth** versus simple scaling, a common pain point for businesses. It also introduces the specific, advanced technique of Appreciative Inquiry (AI).

Case Study 4: The E-Commerce Trap of Uncontrolled Growth

A rapidly expanding regional e-commerce company, focused on specialized home goods, seemed to be living the dream. Over two quarters, they experienced a massive, exciting surge in demand, the kind of explosive growth that makes investors cheer. The leadership was so focused on capturing this momentum that they responded by aggressively ramping up marketing and sales with the singular goal of hitting the numbers.

Within weeks, the organization began to crack under the strain. This external success quickly created internal chaos. Customer service response times tripled, leaving customers frustrated and loyal buyers questioning their choices. Worse, fulfillment errors and mis-ships increased by a catastrophic 40%. The company was successfully selling products, but it was failing to deliver them efficiently or back them up with service.

Leadership had focused entirely on the easy win—external growth—without ever truthfully assessing or strengthening their internal capacity and processes. They were building a massive house on a weak foundation.

The CEO, realizing they were on the verge of turning a success story into a disastrous collapse, made the crucial decision to pause all further sales expansion. This pivot was difficult and counter-intuitive, but necessary. They shifted their focus from pushing products to healing the organization.

Instead of launching a painful, punitive audit over what went wrong, the CEO brought the entire organization together for a transformational Appreciative Inquiry (AI) session. This positive, strength-based framework allowed the team to identify not their weaknesses, but their key strengths and the moments when they had delivered best.

This collaborative process quickly and safely uncovered the critical internal bottlenecks: fragmented inventory management systems and poor cross-departmental communication between sales and the warehouse.

Using these insights, the company made targeted, low-cost internal investments. They funded intensive team training, implemented scalable automation tools to verify shipments, and restructured their warehouse shift schedules based on real data from the AI sessions.

The results were immediate and transformative. Within three months, fulfillment accuracy improved by a stunning 35%, and customer satisfaction scores rose back above industry benchmarks. The company was then able to resume its aggressive growth strategy, this time with confidence, control, and a solid operational foundation.

The Takeaway. This case proves that internal readiness must precede external expansion. Growth that outpaces internal capacity is not success; it is a self-inflicted crisis. Before chasing the next sale, start strengthening the engine that delivers it.

Summary

Scaling a business does not begin with sales or technology. It begins with a mindset shift. The most powerful growth comes from systematically unlocking what is already inside your organization.

1. **Change is Necessary—and It Starts with Listening.** Dysfunction doesn't disappear. It hides. Leaders who engage their teams and act on what they hear build resilient organizations.
2. **People are the Secret to Sustainable Scaling.** Your team holds the answers to your toughest challenges. When people are aligned, engaged, and supported, they become the engine of exponential growth.
3. **Preparation is Everything.** Scaling without internal readiness leads to chaos. By focusing on auditing capacity, committing to discipline, and leveraging Appreciative Inquiry, you can grow with confidence and control.

The answers are in the building. The opportunity is already within your reach. Now it is time to act.

CHAPTER 2
IT STARTS WITH YOU

Stepping into the role of CEO, especially at a company poised for significant growth, is exhilarating. The air thickens with talk of expansion, innovation, and ambitious plans. All that expectation can be intoxicating. It jolts you with energy. And so, you give in to the pressure to deliver quick wins, secure a major deal, or launch a splashy new product.

Yet, you must recognize the profound truth that will dictate your entire tenure: before any structure can rise to meet those ambitions, the foundation must be solid.

This chapter's message is simple but profound: meaningful, lasting change—whether in culture, operations, or strategy—must be modeled at the top. As the CEO, your every action, every subtle sigh, and every choice of where you spend your time sets the tone for the entire organization.

Too often, new leaders feel forced to chase external momentum (external momentum meaning such things as market trends, investor pressure, and competition). But the true, costly challenges—broken processes, leaking revenue, fractured culture—remain hidden beneath the surface, waiting to destabilize even the most brilliant strategy.

Your first responsibility is not to chase external momentum. It is to slow down and truly understand how your company functions from the inside. Obsess over the details. Get the house in order. Only then can you build something that lasts—an empire built on rock, not sand.

The Mandate of Stabilization

This is the first, imperative command for the leader of a high-growth company: before you can build an empire, you must get the house in order. Your job is not to start growing immediately; it is to systematically locate and repair the critical failures. Find where the revenue is leaking, where processes are broken, and where the culture is fractured.

Chasing a higher top-line number while the foundation is crumbling is a blueprint for catastrophic failure. Success in your first year will be measured by stability and efficiency, not speed.

Confronting the Full Truth and Isolation

The transition into the CEO role is often accompanied by an unwelcome revelation. The full truth of a company's dysfunction is rarely revealed in the interview process. The glossy vision quickly gives way to a messy reality where chaos is the norm, hidden by layers of unsustainable, if often heroic effort. The issues are often structural, hitting core processes that fail under stress:

- **Systemic Dysfunction.** You discover a critical mismatch: your sales department promises 48-hour delivery, but fulfillment is designed for 72 hours. This isn't a personnel issue; it is a systemic breakdown that leads to constant customer churn and internal finger-pointing. The customer does not see the chaos—they just leave, taking their lifetime

of value with them, wasting the years spent by your sales department cultivating their patronage.
- **Hidden Costs and Cultural Erosion.** The financials appear healthy until you realize the organization operates with poor accountability. This leads to uncontrolled spending, neglected accounts receivable, and a silent acceptance of slippage—minor errors and delays that collectively drain massive amounts of cash flow. Worse, this lack of accountability breeds cynicism, fracturing the culture from the inside.

This shock is compounded by the isolation of command. You lead an entire organization without an internal peer for high-level counsel, which forces you to process painful truths on your own while simultaneously projecting confidence and clarity. This is the ultimate test of leadership. For you cannot delegate the burden of responsibility. It is ultimately yours to bear.

The problems you face are not roadblocks. They are the raw materials to build your legacy. Your willingness to seek objective truth, rather than chase easy wins, is the first and most critical test of your tenure.

The Three Mistakes of the Stabilization Phase

A leader committed to stabilization often falters not in intention, but in execution. The stabilization mandate is simple in theory, but its success hinges on avoiding three critical mistakes that sabotage the so-called *deep dive* and that reinforce the very dysfunctions you are trying to eliminate.

Mistake 1: The Report Review Illusion

The first mistake is confusing the reviewing of polished reports with a thorough, hands-on audit. When you ask a department head for an operational status report, you rarely receive objective truth; you receive a narrative filtered by ego, fear, and departmental bias. A CEO who limits their audit to reading these documents is operating under an illusion of control.

- **The Correct Action.** You must personally lead the diagnostic phase by what is called *walking the process*. This means sitting down with the front-line teams, observing the material flow, and tracking a customer order from inception to delivery. This is where you find the friction—the precise moments where value is destroyed and errors are introduced. This data that will never appear in a PowerPoint presentation.

Mistake 2: The Hero Fix

This occurs when the CEO, eager to prove their decisiveness, swoops in to solve a major, visible operational breakdown with a unilateral, top-down mandate. While briefly satisfying, the **Hero Fix** undermines the long-term goal of building a self-correcting culture.

- **The Correct Action.** True stabilization requires you to solve the system, not the symptom. When a process breaks, your intervention should not be a solution, but a question: "What information, training, or authority did the team lack that caused this failure, and how do we change the process so the team can fix it themselves next time?" This shifts your role from firefighter to architect of resilience.

Mistake 3: Delegating the Cultural Audit

Many leaders correctly delegate operational deep dives to COOs or consultants, but they mistakenly believe they can delegate the cultural audit as well. Culture is a shadow of the leader. When you outsource its diagnosis, you miss the opportunity to model the vulnerability and curiosity required for true cultural change.

- **The Correct Action.** The cultural assessment must be led by you. This involves structured, confidential listening sessions across all levels. Your job is to absorb the full truth —the cynicism, the hidden costs of fear, and the whispers of broken trust—and model a new way of engaging. Only your vulnerability can grant the organization permission to be honest.

Expanding Pillar 1: The Tactics of Modeling

The CEO's personal conduct is the true culture manual, but modeling the standard requires more than just good intentions; it requires disciplined, repeatable tactics that reinforce your new mandate.

The Discipline of the Clock

Your time management is the clearest indication of what you value. If your calendar is 90% consumed by urgent, tactical meetings, your team internalizes that chaos is the priority. If your calendar shows non-negotiable blocks for strategic planning, leadership development, and walk-the-process time, that sends a powerful signal of intentionality. You must ruthlessly protect your strategic time from the tyranny of the urgent.

The Power of Follow-Through

Inconsistency at the top creates mistrust throughout the ranks. This is particularly damaging during a stabilization period where trust is already fragile. Every commitment you make—no matter how small, whether it's following up on a front-line suggestion or delivering a promised piece of software—becomes a contract of trust. When you follow through, accountability spreads organically. When you fail, the organization assumes the slack is acceptable, leading to that silent acceptance of slippage that erodes cash flow.

The Vocabulary of Accountability

You must eliminate the language of blame and replace it with the language of accountability and process. When something goes wrong, a reactive leader asks, "Who is responsible?" A proactive leader asks, "Where did the process fail, and what is the next action we will take to prevent this from recurring?"

This shift in vocabulary redefines failure as a data point, not a moral failing, and empowers the team to solve the system, not hide the mistake. This empathy-driven approach to accountability is the single greatest tool for healing a fractured culture and eliminating internal finger-pointing.

The Strategic Mindset: Seeing Opportunity

Before any meaningful action can be taken, a leader must first recognize the opportunity for action. This is not blind optimism; it is a clear-eyed mindset that creates a strong foundation for growth. By action we mean a hard shift from defensive problem-solving to aggressive opportunity-finding. This shift is essential to achieve true, sustainable scale.

It is human nature to focus on problems. But by focusing on problems, you often only find more problems. If you focus on solutions, you build momentum. Building an innovative culture begins by shifting focus away from symptoms (challenges) and toward fundamental, growth-oriented questions that define purpose. These questions include:

- Who buys the company's products or services? To find the answer, define the ideal, profitable customer, and where to deploy energy.
- What lessons were learned from recent projects? To find the answer, leverage organizational wisdom to avoid repeating costly mistakes.
- What truly matters to our customers? To find the answer, identify the non-negotiable value proposition that justifies a company's existence.

The answers to these questions transform perceived obstacles into tangible possibilities, guiding teams toward a future filled with potential. The most effective leaders recognize when previous strategies have failed and understand that stagnation is the enemy of growth. Setting aside ego to embrace fresh thinking is crucial.

Actively seeking diversity of thought—whether from the board or a front-line employee—unlocks the discoveries that shape the future. The CEO's job is not to have all the answers, but to ensure the right people and the right questions are in the room.

The Foundational Playbook: Three Pillars of Stability

The path forward is clear and defined: before you can build an empire, you must get your house in order. This stabilization playbook rests on three pillars of execution that will define your first 100 days.

Pillar 1: Model the Standard: Leadership

The CEO is always visible and operates in a perpetual spotlight. Every employee watches how you react to crisis, who you hire, and, most importantly, how you govern yourself. Your personal conduct is the true culture manual.

- **The Power of Signals.** Your first moves are signals that indicate who you are as a CEO. Every decision is magnified. You must set the tone for the organization by being impeccably disciplined. If you champion work-life balance but routinely send non-urgent emails at 11:00 PM, the organization internalizes the hypocrisy, creating stress and the obligation to follow suit. Your actions, not your memos, define the standard operating procedure.
- **Walk the Talk.** Model accountability and positive leadership. Follow through on every commitment, no matter how small, as inconsistency at the top creates mistrust throughout the ranks. Serve your employees with empathy and authenticity. When employees feel valued by their leader, they take ownership of their results, and accountability spreads organically, requiring far less formal structure or punitive oversight.

Pillar 2: Transform Governance into Partnership: The Board

The CEO is often isolated from the day-to-day of the company. They are alone in their role. This often becomes a problem. The solution is strategic relationship building. You must engage often and deeply with your Board of Directors, treating them not as auditors, but as your external, objective peer group.

- **Transform Oversight.** Your Board is a collective of experienced, objective peers who have successfully navigated similar crises and who have successfully scaled businesses. They are your external brain trust. Turn board meetings into working sessions where you present honestly the internal dysfunctions you've discovered, complete with solutions. This demonstrates transparency and your confidence in your plan.

- **Gain Counsel.** By actively inviting their strategic input on stabilization such as asking for advice on managing investor expectations during a period of internal focus or structuring a rapid operational review—you unlock external perspective and wisdom. You transform the board from a potential critic into a powerful ally, converting the loneliness of command into a powerful alliance for change.

Pillar 3: Conduct a Deep Dive into Operations: Action

You must personally lead this effort. This goes far beyond reviewing reports. It requires mapping the actual work being done to hunt out friction and waste.

- **Slow Down to Speed Up.** Take time to thoroughly understand how every part of the company functions. This is the diagnostic phase. Physically walk through the processes: sit with the team that handles receivables; track a customer order from click to delivery. You are hunting for friction—the precise points where value is being destroyed and errors are introduced. Only by pinpointing the leak can you repair the system.
- **Front-Line Insights.** Do not rely solely on managers and polished reports. Spend time with the front-line employees; their insights are gold. They know exactly why the software is bypassed, why inventory is miscounted, and why customers are frustrated. This investigative work is crucial for gathering the granular data needed to counter internal resistance to change. The time spent stabilizing operations now will be repaid tenfold in predictable, controlled growth later.

The Strategic Imperatives of Proactive Leadership

The mandate to slow down, look inward, and focus on stabilization is not merely a defensive measure—it is the most strategic path to high, sustainable growth. Having achieved foundational stability, the CEO's next challenge is to shift the organization's energy from crisis management to intentional foresight.

The Cost of Chaos: The Reactive Trap

When a leader fails to prioritize stability and forward vision, the company falls into a costly cycle of reactivity. This is the trap where you are perpetually defined by external events. Teams spend a disproportionate amount of time fighting fires. This leads to stress, finger-pointing, and cultural erosion. The environment becomes defined by firefighting, not execution.

The greatest damage is anxiety, not the momentum it creates. When you lead from instinct alone, you leave your people in a constant state of reaction, always guessing what's next. Because the CEO's intentions are unclear, every pivot feels arbitrary, breeding cynicism and sapping productive energy.

The solution is to change your leadership strategy so that you are defined by design, not events. You must replace the anxiety of reaction with the clarity of direction.

1. Lead with Intention and Foresight

Leadership is not a spontaneous endeavor. The most successful CEOs lead with purpose, not just impulse. Every major decision must align with a clearly articulated mission.

- **The Power of Today's Focus.** The ability to predict the future requires an acute awareness of what is happening *today*. True foresight is a rigorous deduction based on

current operations and market signals. You must ruthlessly prioritize and focus only on what matters today so that you have the bandwidth to look to the future. Eliminate the noise, delegate the non-essential, and concentrate your energy on stabilizing the core.
- **Predicting and Positioning.** To truly shape the destiny of a business, you must be able to anticipate tomorrow and position the business accordingly. The proactive leader asks: "Based on our current operational stability and market signals, how must we adjust our foundation today—in terms of talent, processes, and capital—to meet the reality of 12 months from now?"

2. The Proactive CEO's Ritual

Successfully transitioning from reaction to proactivity requires implementing new daily disciplines that dedicate time, communication, and a perspective on the future.

- **Prioritize Strategic Planning.** Do not allow your calendar to be consumed by crisis. Instead dedicate non-negotiable time to proactive strategy sessions. This is a commitment to working *on* the business, not just *in* it. Decisively shift focus from reacting to planning.
- **Communicate Clear Intentions.** A reactive company is a confused company. You must make your goals, priorities, and expectations explicit. Provide clarity and predictability in your leadership. When you clearly articulate *why* you are making a move, whether it's slowing growth to fix a process or investing in a new technology—you empower your team to align their daily tasks with your long-term vision.
- **Seek Outside Perspectives.** To avoid falling back into reactive patterns, routinely invite feedback from trusted advisors, board members, or external experts. Use their

objective insights to challenge your own assumptions and eliminate the internal bias that leads to stagnation.

3. The Proactive CEO's Ritual: Beyond the Calendar

The strategic leader dedicates non-negotiable time to work *on* the business, replacing anxiety with clarity.

- **The Weekly Strategic White Space**
  - The CEO must establish a mandatory, three-hour white-space session once a week dedicated solely to proactive strategy (a white-space is an unexplored or unserved market area). This time is for thinking, anticipating, and positioning, and is immune to crisis intervention.
  - During this session, the leader must ask and answer the critical question: "Based on our current operational stability and market signals, how must we adjust our foundation today—in terms of talent, processes, and capital—to meet the reality of 12 months from now?"
  - By ritualizing foresight, you shift your leadership from being defined by events to being defined by design.
- **The Intentional Communication Loop**
  - A reactive company is a confused company. You must replace the anxiety of reaction with the clarity of direction.
  - This is achieved through an intentional communication loop where your goals, priorities, and expectations are made explicit.
  - When you clearly articulate *why* you are making a move —whether it is slowing growth to fix a process or investing in a new technology, you empower your team to align their daily tasks with your long-term vision.
  - This communication must be redundant, simple, and

consistent, ensuring that the purpose of the pause (stabilization) is as clear as the eventual goal (scaling).

The Strategic Imperative: Capacity as Competitive Advantage

The ultimate return on this stabilization effort is the transformation of your internal capacity from a bottleneck into a competitive advantage. When systems are streamlined, people are empowered, and communication is clear. As well, your company can absorb external shocks and manage increased volume with grace. This is the definition of resilient growth.

In the market, speed is often prioritized over stamina. Your competitors will likely fall into the growth trap, chasing sales without first building capacity. Their high-growth phase will be punctuated by chaos, high turnover, and poor customer experience.

By contrast, your disciplined, stable organization—with its low internal friction and high accountability—will be able to deploy capital, introduce new products, and integrate acquisitions with a level of control and predictability that is impossible to copy.

Your internal discipline is what will differentiate your company. This stability ensures that when you finally unleash your lead generation engine, the resulting growth will be profitable, sustainable, and truly exponential.

Why This Works: Compounding Returns

Leading with intention is the most significant strategic investment a CEO can make. Why? Because it delivers critical, compounding returns for the organization:

- **Build Lasting Solutions.** Obsessing over details addresses the root problems thus setting the stage for truly

sustainable growth rather than on transient surges in sales built on shaky ground.
- **Empower High-Performing Teams.** Modeling accountability and consistently communicating intentions enables your employees to act with confidence and purpose. This fosters a powerful culture of trust and organic accountability where the team takes ownership.
- **Position for Strategic Advantage.** Anticipating future opportunities and challenges ensures your business is strategically aligned and ready to seize new possibilities, thus guaranteeing growth that endures beyond the current business cycle.

Real-Life Examples: The Proactive Transformation

The efficacy of seeking answers within your organization is not mere theory; it is a set of principles. And these principles are behind some of the most dramatic and successful corporate turnarounds of our era.

This section steps out of the mid-market and onto the global stage, showcasing how incumbent leaders faced down existential threats by deliberately pausing external pursuit to master internal operations.

From cultural reinvention at a tech giant to the systemic overhaul of a manufacturing behemoth, and even to a leader's personal quest for mastery, these stories prove the powerful truth that internal alignment is the precondition for sustained market domination. The choice is simple: proactively fix your house or eventually pay the catastrophic price.

Real-Life Story: Satya Nadella and the Microsoft Turnaround

When Satya Nadella took the helm as CEO of Microsoft in 2014, he did not inherit a failing startup—he inherited a corporate behemoth struggling with systemic stagnation and an existential identity crisis. The company, once the undisputed leader of the tech world, was rapidly losing relevance in the new mobile and cloud computing markets. Internally, the culture was characterized by deep, poisonous silos—departmental rivalries were fierce, innovation was stifled, and a pervasive fixed mindset meant employees focused more on defending their turf than on collective success. The internal atmosphere was, by many accounts, dysfunctional and combative.

The conventional external playbook would have called for immediate, aggressive acquisition and cost-cutting measures, chasing new market share—what is rightly identified as *the growth trap*. Instead, Nadella demonstrated profound strategic discipline by relentlessly focusing inward, prioritizing the core mandate: get the house in order.

His first action was not a massive reorganization; it was an empathetic assessment of the company's reality. He challenged the organization to shift its narrative from one of past glory and internal competition to one of radical, honest self-reflection. He famously asked fundamental, internal questions: Why do we exist? What value do we add that only we can provide? What can we learn from our past failures?

Nadella explicitly recognized that the transformation required a fundamental cultural shift from a *fixed mindset* (believing intelligence is static) to a *growth mindset* (believing intelligence and skill can be developed through effort). He didn't just mandate this shift; he modeled it from the top, pushing empathy, curiosity, learning, and accountability to become the company's new currency.

To enable this, he systematically broke down the debilitating internal silos that had been choking collaboration. Furthermore, he strategically engaged with the board, transforming them from distant, skeptical overseers into proactive strategic partners focused on long-term vision. This top-to-bottom alignment was critical to steering the massive organization in a radically new direction.

This stabilization-first, cultural-centric approach laid the essential foundation. It transformed Microsoft's fractured culture, reignited internal innovation, and ultimately fueled the company's resurgence as the dominant leader in cloud computing (Azure). By fixing the core culture, Nadella proved that internal alignment is the precondition for sustainable market domination.

General Motors and the Culture of Proactivity

In 2014, when Mary Barra took the reins as CEO of General Motors (GM), she immediately inherited a catastrophic recall crisis due to the failure of ignition switches. This crisis exposed deep, systemic flaws within the organization. The crisis wasn't just about a technical defect. That technical defect was a symptom of a deeply reactive, insular culture where mistakes were hidden, accountability was diffused, and internal silos prevented crucial safety information from reaching the top. Barra's key challenge was not to fix cars, but to fix the organization's mindset and its machinery of leadership.

Instead of allowing the organization to remain trapped in a crisis-response cycle, Barra focused on forcing a proactive mindset through deliberate, structural changes to the company's internal rhythm. She understood that culture follows structure.

Her success was due to her focus on three mandates. In these mandates she:

- **Prioritized Strategy over Tactics (The Structural Change).** Barra initiated regular, mandatory, and dedicated strategy sessions focused squarely on anticipating future risks and opportunities, rather than the immediate fire drills of the day. This dedication of time to foresight was the key structural change. It mandated that leaders spend time

on what *might* happen next, not just what was currently on fire, fundamentally shifting resource allocation toward prevention and innovation.
- **Communicated Intention for Clarity (The Cultural Shift).** Barra prioritized commitment to safety and quality above all else. And she made her priorities and intentions crystal clear to every employee from the CFO to the line workers. This transparency was a vital course-correction. By communicating openly, she empowered frontline teams to act with purpose and to stop deferring decisions or hiding potential issues out of fear. She replaced confusion with clear marching orders.
- **Challenged Legacy Assumptions (The Accountability Tool).** She invited feedback from both internal technical teams and external safety experts, publicly challenging legacy assumptions and long-held "rules" that had fostered the reactive culture. By encouraging a culture of proactive problem-solving and radical honesty, she injected accountability into every layer of decision-making.

By structurally shifting GM's leadership approach from a perpetual state of reaction to one of strategic proactivity, Barra helped restore consumer and internal trust. More importantly, she successfully positioned the company to tackle future-forward challenges, such as the pivot to electric vehicles, and in doing so she demonstrated that a healthy internal culture is the ultimate foundation for sustainable growth and innovation.

The Leader's Deep Dive – Winning the MVP

The lesson that internal focus drives external success applies not only to multi-billion-dollar companies but also, at the personal level, to the leader themselves.

In October 2023, I (Jeff) made a decision that felt strategically uncomfortable: I joined a competitive local Pool League despite having virtually no experience. This wasn't a hobby. It was a conscious, personal challenge—a deliberate move to step outside my comfort zone and force a period of intense learning and focus, which I framed as my personal *Deep Dive into Operations*.

The initial phase was predictable and profoundly humbling. I was facing experienced players, but my skills at pool were non-existent. And so, I focused. I practiced the fundamentals relentlessly—grip, stance, stroke, and English—and ignored the scores and the outcomes. This was analogous to a business leader pausing outward expansion to focus solely on perfecting their company's core process and culture.

Fast forward to the 2025 Spring League. After months of setting aside my ego and dedicating myself to the process, I found myself playing with a level of control, strategic foresight, and composure I had never imagined possible.

The reward for this internal focus came in the form of external recognition: I ultimately won the 2025 Spring League MVP Award for Nine-Ball—an award based not just on wins (I won 83% of my matches that season), but on demonstrated, sustained improvement and strategic execution.

The experience holds a critical reminder for every executive and business owner: growth starts when the comfort zone ends. If you, as the leader, do not push yourself into areas of uncertainty and if you do not humbly engage in a personal deep dive, you will never truly learn the depth of resilience, skill, and creative problem-solving that your organization—or you, as its guiding force—are truly capable of accomplishing. The principles you apply to your P&L statement must first be applied to your own development.

Summary

This chapter establishes that meaningful, lasting change begins and ends with the CEO's intentional mindset.

The leader's first imperative is the **Foundational Mandate,** that is to slow down and build a solid foundation before chasing external momentum. This is achieved by modeling accountability, leveraging the board of directors as a powerful resource, and conducting a deep dive to address hidden dysfunctions.

Ultimately, the CEO must embrace the **Proactive Advantage**. By dedicating time to strategic planning and communicating clear intentions, the leader breaks cycles of stagnation, empowers teams with clarity, and strategically positions the organization for enduring success.

The journey to exponential growth is founded on the decisions you make today. By replacing the anxiety of reaction with the momentum of purpose, you stop being busy and start being impactful.

The next chapter will show you how to take that strong, stable foundation and translate it into a compelling vision behind which the entire organization can mobilize.

CHAPTER 3
EFFECTIVE LEADERSHIP: THE ENGINE OF SCALE

When organizations chase growth, they often look outward—seeking new strategies, revolutionary technologies, or external experts promising a quick fix. They invest millions in market analysis and competitive intelligence yet frequently overlook the most potent force for sustained competitive advantage.

The real leverage point for sustainable success is already inside your building, it is found in your people, your culture, and, most importantly, your leadership. Leadership is the single most critical lever determining whether your organization's potential is realized or squandered.

The styles and behaviors modeled from the top set the tone for every decision, every process, and every interpersonal interaction that follows. It is the core operating system of the entire organization. When this system is outdated or flawed, no amount of external investment can compensate for internal friction, chaos, and lost potential.

The Crisis of Top-Down Control

The failures of modern leadership are rooted in a single, outdated paradigm: **Top-Down Leadership,** which mistakenly equates absolute control with competence and operational success. This rigid reliance on hierarchy chokes the flow of vital information, delays necessary adjustments, and ultimately stifles the very creativity and speed needed for scalable growth.

The leader, isolated by title and surrounded by layers of fearful reporting, inevitably becomes the biggest, most expensive bottleneck in the system.

The Pitfalls of Command and Compliance

The destructive behaviors modeled at the top, such as suffocating micromanagement, opaque top-down decision-making, and a punitive error culture are the silent killers of scale. This archaic approach insists that the leader is the smartest person in the room, a dangerous mindset that guarantees intellectual stagnation for both the leader and the organization.

The communication model is rigidly linear. The leader speaks; others listen. This is not dialogue; it is dictation, and it guarantees that bad news travels slowly, if at all.

When leaders rely on this command-and-control style, they receive compliance, not commitment. Employees become like cogs in a machine. They follow orders to avoid repercussions, and not because they're intellectually or emotionally invested in the outcome of the orders.

This lack of emotional ownership is profoundly corrosive. Problems slip through the cracks not because the staff lacks competence, but because it's not the employee's reputation on the line. The incentive structure becomes purely defensive: minimize visibility, avoid error, and wait for the boss to give the next instruction.

This constant, unnecessary intervention stifles personal initiative, signals a deep-seated mistrust in the staff's capabilities, and effectively trains the team to wait passively for the next rescue. As the cliché goes—and it is the truth—people do not leave companies, they leave bad managers.

No external incentive system, no motivational slogan, and no sophisticated strategic pivot can ever compensate for the systemic damage caused by poor, centralized leadership. This is a tax on talent that leads to high turnover and a guarantee of organizational mediocrity.

The Strategic Blindness to the Why

This top-down environment actively stifles creativity and suffocates new ideas, making employees unwilling to contribute their valuable intellectual capital. The granular knowledge possessed by the front-line staff, the true operational reality of customer complaints, system flaws, and process inefficiencies, is essentially locked away, creating an invisible, yet massive, data deficit at the executive level. This structural information failure is far more damaging than any market fluctuation.

This leads to a hidden crisis that routinely derails high-potential companies. Many companies generate substantial revenue but ultimately fail to grow profitably due to operational dysfunction. The brutal irony is that the leader knows the *what*—the poor financial results, shrinking margins, high turnover, and stagnant innovation shown on the balance sheet—but is tragically blind to the *why*.

Financial statements only show the "what," not the "why," and the "why" resides in the operational realities that the top-down structure has systematically ignored. The leader's rigid insistence on control isolates them from the very truth required to fix the business.

When genuine growth hits, this structural blindness, rooted in the top-down paradigm, guarantees organizational chaos and unmanageable complexity.

Leaders Who Inspire: The Shift to Co-Creation

The crisis created by **Top-Down Control** has a powerful and necessary antidote: the intentional shift toward collaborative leadership. This is more than a management tweak. It is a fundamental change in philosophy.

You must stop trying to manage people and start focusing on inspiring and influencing them. Remember this crucial distinction: you manage projects and budgets; you lead people. Managing people implies controlling their actions. Leading people implies unlocking their potential.

True leadership is not about claiming to have all the answers. This is a futile and isolating task. Instead, true leadership is about asking the right questions and about knowing *who* to ask.

It is the discipline of leveraging collective intelligence, recognizing that the sharpest, most resilient solutions are generated when authority is distributed, and every voice contributes to the strategic outcome. This is the difference between dictation and co-creation.

From Prescription to Co-Creation

Collaborative leaders are exponentially more successful than top-down ones. Grasping this fundamental premise is crucial for sustainable growth. Great leaders replace the habit of issuing orders for change with a disciplined inquiry. They pose strategic, open-ended questions that challenge assumptions and force the entire team to co-create solutions. These questions act as probes, forcing knowledge—the true power—to surface.

This simple act of asking better questions and letting the team find the answers, is a monumental transfer of trust and ownership. It signals, unequivocally, that the leader trusts the team's competence to solve complex problems, validating their expertise. By systematically valuing the granular knowledge held by frontline staff and middle managers, leaders transform passive compliance into active contribution.

Change is no longer a mandate handed down. It becomes a shared mission team members help design, leading to intrinsic buy-in. This ownership acts as a powerful cultural firewall, drastically increasing the speed of implementation and the long-term sustainability of the changes. This is because the solutions are operationally resilient and internally championed.

The Leader on the Sidelines: Trading Intervention for Influence

We often encounter leaders whose default to jumping *on the field* to solve every crisis, mistakenly believing this reinforces their value as the Chief Problem-Solver.

This behavior can become addictive, and it shows a failure to delegate. The true, strategic role of the great leader is on the sidelines, acting as the coach, the strategist, and the chief enabler of the team's success.

When the leader steps back, they gain a crucial strategic perspective. They rise above the noise of daily urgencies and can observe the entire system at work, identifying operational friction points invisible to those deep in the fray.

This psychological and structural shift empowers the team to develop mastery and true accountability. By allowing employees to navigate and own the complexity of their work, they build the muscle memory and decision-making capability essential for scaling.

Delegating tactical execution is not abdication. It is the highest form of trust and the most powerful leverage point for scaling, as it preserves the leader's bandwidth for critical strategic oversight—tasks like anticipating market shifts, securing capital, and building future organizational capacity.

The Heartbeat of Authentic Dialogue

Collaboration is utterly impossible without genuine, free-flowing communication that transcends hierarchy. The consistent, intentional internal communication fostered by inspirational leaders is the heartbeat of a thriving organization and the necessary foundation of psychological safety for all employees.

These leaders don't just broadcast mandates. They facilitate dialogue and strategically hold conversations *before* any major launch, ensuring ideas and concerns are aired when they can still shape the outcome. This process signals to every employee that their input is not only welcome but essential, replacing the stifling silence of fear with the dynamic energy of shared ownership.

One of the most powerful tools in this authentic dialogue is Appreciative Inquiry (AI). Transformative leaders utilize AI to fundamentally shift the organizational focus away from its deficiencies and toward its strengths. Instead of initiating change by asking, "What problems do we need to fix?" AI asks, "What works incredibly well here, and how can we do a lot more of it?"

This methodology engages people at every level, turning the organizational energy away from chronic failures and building solutions exclusively on a foundation of proven success. This strategic, positive reframing naturally fosters optimism, accelerates successful change implementation, and dramatically increases psychological safety, allowing teams to envision a better future based on their own successful history.

Furthermore, in moments of crisis or profound challenge, a leader's character is forged by their communication. The highest level of communication demands transparency and trust. Leaders who take responsibility, own their decisions, and openly admit mistakes are not weak; they are building unshakeable authenticity and trust.

This willingness to show vulnerability, to say, "We made a mistake, and I am accountable" can swiftly dismantle the pervasive, toxic culture of blame and unify the team around a collective, honest path forward. This act of facing the unvarnished truth together proves that resilience is built on shared reality and integrity, making the leader worthy of loyalty.

The ROI of Empowerment: Action and Returns

The shift from the control-based model to collaborative leadership is far more than a cultural initiative. It is a profound strategic and financial imperative. This transformation delivers compounding returns to your business, fundamentally changing the relationship between people and profit.

By empowering your teams, you transform employee engagement from an abstract ideal into hard performance metrics that directly and measurably improve the bottom line, multiply enterprise value, and secure long-term competitive advantage. When employees move from being *managed resources* to being *valued owners* of the outcome, their discretionary effort becomes the most reliable engine for sustainable growth.

This investment yields dividends that are both immediate—in the form of faster decision-making and reduced waste—and long-term, through increased innovation and lower talent turnover.

Operationalizing Collaboration

To successfully make this shift, leaders must commit to embedding specific actions into their daily routine:

1. **Shift to Dialogue.** Start conversations by asking questions, not giving orders. Instead of declaring a solution, frame the problem as a shared challenge. Prioritize consistent internal communication that ensures everyone understands the "why," thus treating internal messages with the same rigor and strategic importance as external marketing campaigns.

2. **Empower Decisions.** Delegate authority for operational decisions to frontline employees, granting them the power to call audibles within their scope of expertise. This strategic move dramatically accelerates problem-solving cycles (reducing resolution time from days to minutes) and validates the employee's critical, on-the-ground knowledge.
3. **Co-Creation.** Rather than issue a mandate, invite employees to co-create solutions to organizational challenges. Solutions designed and vetted by the people who perform the work are inherently more effective, durable, and sustainable, requiring significantly less management enforcement and follow-up.
4. **Share the Spotlight.** Recognize contributions publicly and give explicit credit to the co-creators of success. By consistently sharing the spotlight, you reinforce the value of contribution and encourage ongoing participation from everyone, regardless of corporate hierarchy. This simple act is a high-return investment in intrinsic motivation.

The Tangible Returns of Collaborative Leadership

The commitment to disciplined inquiry and empowerment does not just create a nicer workplace. It yields powerful, measurable, and highly tangible business returns. First and foremost, collaborative leadership is the key to unlocking potential and ownership. While top-down authority stifles creativity and encourages intellectual retreat, collaborative environments actively empower ownership, leading directly to better, faster, and more innovative solutions alongside significantly higher morale. The commitment generated by a co-created solution is exponentially stronger than mere passive compliance, effectively leveraging the organization's collective intellectual capital to solve problems in ways the leadership alone never could.

This ownership translates directly into driving profitability. By empowering frontline staff to identify and act on the inefficiencies they see firsthand, the organization increases its agility and drives grassroots operational excellence.

This process where employees address the flaws in their daily work helps organizations grow profitably by addressing the hidden "why" behind performance issues—that is, the systemic problems that financial reports alone are incapable of revealing. This employee engagement acts as an invaluable form of risk mitigation, turning internal oversight into a function of the entire workforce.

Finally, this approach guarantees sustainable change. Co-creating solutions builds intrinsic buy-in and leverages the collective wisdom across all levels of the business. This ensures that when a change is implemented, it is not only theoretically sound but is championed by the entire organization.

This widespread endorsement makes the solution stick long-term, dramatically reducing the costly churn, resistance, and rework that inevitably plague initiatives that are mandated from the top down. Collaborative solutions are resilient solutions.

The "Undercover Boss" Approach to Intelligence Gathering

The first and most critical step when implementing the framework of *The Answers Are in the Building* is for the leader to trade the commander's chair for the observer's lens. The value of stepping off the sidelines—of truly immersing oneself in the day-to-day operations—is best seen when it yields immediate, actionable intelligence that formal channels deliberately obscure.

This is the strategic value of the "Undercover Boss" approach—not just as a public relations stunt, but as a deliberate, covert method to gather authentic, unvarnished operational intelligence. By working anonymously on the front line for a defined period, the leader bypasses the natural inclination of employees to put on a show for visitors.

This approach yields the kind of unfiltered feedback about process friction, waste, and ingenious solutions that would never, under any circumstances, surface in a staged boardroom review, a formalized suggestion box, or a top-down survey.

Consider a leader who observes a cashier working the register. Frustrated by a clunky, multi-step software requirement that takes valuable time, the employee has created their own simple, unauthorized solution—perhaps a unique keyboard shortcut sequence or a small physical process hack—to streamline the checkout and speed up the line. This local, grassroots innovation, born of necessity and frustration, is the hidden answer.

Through this brief but deliberate observation, the leader immediately gains a superior, practical innovation that, when scaled across all locations, can save valuable minutes per transaction company-wide, potentially equating to millions in annual efficiency gains.

More importantly than financial gain, the leader gains a profound cultural tool: co-creation. By formally inviting that cashier to present their grassroots innovation to headquarters—not as a compliant worker, but as a recognized expert, the leader not only adopts a superior solution but fundamentally transforms the employee's relationship with the company.

It proves, beyond a shadow of a doubt, that the most practical, scalable, and profitable answers for the business truly lie within the existing expertise and ingenuity of its own people. This is how you shift from managing tasks to cultivating innovation.

Supportive Leadership: The Protective Filter

After exploring the shift to collaborative dialogue, it is essential to focus on the specific, protective traits that distinguish truly effective leaders—those rooted in actively supporting and shielding their teams. This supportive discipline is the final, crucial component of building a scalable, high-performance culture.

The Shift from Reactive to Anticipatory

Many leaders rely on quick-thinking and adaptability as their main strategy, mistakenly believing that operational planning is just a simple to-do list. This reactive approach leads to constant, exhausting firefighting and overwhelms teams with preventable crises. This depletes morale, increases stress, and leaves no bandwidth for innovation or strategic growth.

Great leaders don't just respond to challenges. They anticipate them. They look ahead, identify potential operational and market obstacles, and prepare their teams to meet them head-on. The most immediate sign of supportive leadership is a team empowered to do meaningful, focused work without constant distraction.

Real leadership isn't about handling crises; it is about making sure crises do not happen in the first place. And real leadership does this by installing proactive systems, redundant checks, and disciplined planning cycles.

The Protective Filter: Protection Over Delegation

Supportive leaders understand that their primary job is to be a filter, not just a delegator. As organizations experience growth, the number of demands and requests—originating from both internal stakeholders and external clients—multiplies exponentially, creating an environment of perpetual distraction.

While a good leader delegates tasks to enable workflow, a great leader protects their teams from this unnecessary noise and unrealistic expectations. They stand as a barrier between the operational team and the chaos of the external environment.

This protection manifests as the strategic use of the word "no" on behalf of their people. By absorbing the external pressure and vetting every incoming request against the team's core objectives, the supportive leader ensures that team energy is directed *only* toward the activities that truly drive innovation and measurable results.

This is a critical investment in efficiency. It prevents valuable time and intellectual capital from being wasted on demands that seem urgent but are in fact low priority. This isn't about hoarding control or creating an echo chamber. It is about respecting the team's time and focus and seeing it as the organization's most finite and valuable resource. By controlling the inflow, the leader maximizes the output.

The Courage of Accountability

Leadership is not about authority. It is not about reminding others of your title. It is about influence, accountability, and having the courage to address difficult issues before they become costly, cultural problems. When leaders avoid tough conversations surrounding poor performance or toxicity, the entire business pays a heavy, quantifiable price.

When leaders lack the courage to address difficult issues, the consequences are immediate and severe, exacting a high cost on the entire business. There is the direct financial toll of lost revenue and profit due to decreased productivity. Poor performance quickly becomes tolerated as does the minimum accepted standard, acting as a brake that slows down the most efficient, high-performing employees.

Secondly, this inaction leads to significantly increased turnover costs. High performers, often the most conscientious and principled employees, become unwilling to carry the perpetual burden of underperforming colleagues, leading them to seek environments where excellence is the norm.

This forces the company into a cycle of costly and continuous recruitment and training. Beyond internal damage, the organization risks damaged client relationships and the potential loss of future business due to unreliable service delivery and unchecked incompetence.

Most insidiously, this avoidance creates a toxic company culture that spreads throughout the organization like a virus, breeding deep resentment and cynicism among the workforce, and ultimately leading to mass disengagement. What you tolerate becomes your culture. True leadership, therefore, means having the courage to build a high-trust environment where everyone is supported, protected, and expected to excel.

Action and Returns of Supportive Leadership

Transforming into a supportive leader requires replacing reactive habits with disciplined, proactive actions that are focused on influence and protection.

The Discipline of Supportive Leadership

Transforming into a supportive leader begins with a conscious choice to lead by influence, not authority. This means making a daily commitment to govern through respect, trust, and shared vision rather than relying on the sheer weight of your hierarchy or title. Instead of demanding obedience, you focus on inspiring true commitment by actively asking for buy-in and consistently valuing the unique expertise of every team member.

This style is intrinsically linked to foresight, compelling you to practice strategic, proactive planning. Dedicate time to anticipating challenges three to six months ahead. Your goal is to proactively dismantle operational roadblocks before they manifest as crises. This immediately minimizes the need for exhausting firefighting and preserves the team's valuable bandwidth for high-value, growth-oriented work.

When managing the daily workflow, you must learn to delegate tasks and act as a filter. While you delegate tasks with full authority to execute and adjust as needed, your primary function is to act as a protective filter, shielding your team from unnecessary noise, distractions, and conflicting priorities. This means protecting the team from distracting requests or unrealistic deadlines that don't align with core objectives, ensuring their focus remains pinpointed on driving essential results.

A supportive culture also demands the courage to address difficult conversations directly and constructively. You must develop the fortitude to engage promptly in necessary conflict. Frame the conversation around setting clear expectations and supporting future growth, thereby preventing small issues from festering into systemic cultural toxicity.

Finally, you must own decisions and mistakes as a leader. Model genuine accountability by taking full responsibility for decisions and openly admitting errors, especially during moments of challenge or crisis. This transparent integrity is the fastest, most powerful way to dismantle a blame culture and encourage the kind of calculated risk-taking that drives innovation throughout the entire organization.

Case Studies

These high-profile case studies validate the power of collaborative and supportive leadership principles, proving their effectiveness in diverse, high-growth environments.

Supportive leadership delivers tangible, measurable benefits to the organization, beginning with the symbiotic effects on loyalty and productivity. An influence-based style of leadership naturally fosters deep loyalty and genuine engagement among team members, which in turn significantly reduces the costly cycle of employee turnover.

Furthermore, when this supportive approach incorporates proactive planning, it minimizes debilitating crises, allowing employees to focus their energy on meaningful, high-value work rather than on perpetual firefighting. This direct alignment of effort leads inevitably to higher productivity and superior organizational outcomes.

This framework is further cemented by the strategic advantages of focus, protection, and innovation. By strategically acting as a filter, the leader shields teams from non-essential demands and distractions. This protection helps team members maintain intense focus, significantly reduces the risk of burnout, and ensures that valuable time is consciously channeled toward activities that truly drive innovation and measurable results. A protected, focused team is one that operates at maximum efficiency.

Crucially, this supportive model is the foundation for trust, accountability, and risk mitigation. The simple discipline of addressing performance issues promptly protects overall productivity and maintains high team morale. Beyond that, the leader's demonstrated authenticity and accountability—their willingness to own mistakes—builds the bedrock of trust within the organization.

This psychological safety fosters a culture where learning is valued over blame, strengthening internal collaboration and external relationships that collectively safeguard the company's reputation and mitigate future risks.

Satya Nadella at Microsoft: The Culture Catalyst

When Satya Nadella took the helm as CEO of Microsoft in 2014, he understood that the company's biggest enemy wasn't a competitor; it was its own internal culture. He recognized that Microsoft's historically competitive, internal, top-down culture—a deep-seated fixed mindset that rewarded turf wars and perfectionism—was actively stifling innovation and leading to market stagnation.

Instead of chasing external acquisitions, Nadella focused relentlessly inward. He championed a profound cultural transformation, shifting the organization from a defensive, entitled know-it-all mentality to a curious, adaptable learn-it-all culture. This wasn't soft leadership; it was an urgent strategic mandate emphasizing empathy, vulnerability, collaboration, and open communication as the new engine of growth.

He specifically and publicly encouraged leaders to ask questions, listen actively, and embrace the principles of Appreciative Inquiry—a strength-based approach—to build upon internal capabilities and successes rather than dwelling solely on perceived deficits and blame. This fundamental leadership transformation, modeled from the top, directly led to increased employee engagement, demolished cross-functional silos, and revitalized innovation.

The result was astonishing. Microsoft's surge in relevance and market value, driven by the success of Azure, proved that culture change is the fastest, most sustainable path to business change. Nadella showed that if the answers are indeed in the building, the leader's primary job is to create psychological safety and structural willingness for those answers to be voiced and acted upon.

Starbucks' Radical Response to Crisis—Owning the Mistake

The ultimate test of a leader's commitment to getting their house in order comes not during a period of smooth growth, but during a profound crisis. Following the highly publicized, racially charged incident in a Philadelphia store in 2018, Starbucks' leadership demonstrated the critical value of radical accountability and vulnerable leadership.

The temptation for a corporation of that size is always to deflect, apologize generically, and minimize the damage to quarterly earnings. Instead, Starbucks' then-CEO Kevin Johnson and his team refused to look outside for easy excuses.

They took immediate, public, and unequivocal accountability, admitting that the incident exposed systemic issues within their company culture and training.

Their response was a dramatic demonstration of prioritizing internal health over external profits. They made the audacious decision to close over 8,000 U.S. company-owned stores for an entire afternoon.

This massive, coordinated event was dedicated to comprehensive employee training focused on unconscious bias and inclusion. This move cost the company millions in lost sales, but it sent a clear signal to both employees and customers: the company was willing to pay a high price to fix the problems within its house.

This open communication, willingness to own a catastrophic mistake, and dedication to investing in internal education helped rebuild trust with employees, stakeholders, and the public. The action proved that authenticity in crisis management—and a bold commitment to fixing the cultural root of the problem—is the fastest, most effective way to unify stakeholders and preserve long-term brand value. They shifted the internal culture from one that tolerated ignorance to one that was accountable for awareness.

Google's TGIF Meetings: The Power of Inquiry

Google's long-standing tradition of weekly all-hands meetings, famously known as TGIF (Thank God It's Friday), is the beating heart of its corporate culture, transforming internal communication from a simple corporate necessity into a powerful strategic asset. It is far more than an update session; it is the arena where radical transparency is consistently practiced and reinforced.

The true genius of TGIF lies in its design as an inquiry-driven, two-way dialogue. Rather than executives simply delivering a top-down mandate, the platform inverts the communication flow. Employees from every corner of the globe and every level of the hierarchy, submit and anonymously upvote the questions that matter most to them. This mechanism ensures that when executives, often including the CEO, step up to the microphone, they are compelled to address the collective, unfiltered voice of the workforce. They must tackle the difficult, sensitive, or challenging topics—from major product pivots and organizational changes to stock performance and ethical controversies.

By consistently tackling these issues head-on, and in a public forum, the company minimizes the spread of rumors and misinformation that can cripple morale and productivity in less open organizations.

This consistent, vulnerable act of openness from leadership fosters an environment where employees feel genuinely heard and respected as essential stakeholders. The validation that comes from having a shared question addressed by the highest level of leadership builds trust and significantly boosts morale and commitment.

Ultimately, this sustained practice of open-door dialogue is what deepens employee investment and ensures strategic alignment. The workforce doesn't just passively receive the company's direction; they are brought into the conversation understanding *what* the strategy is, *why* it is necessary, and *what* challenges lie ahead.

This deep understanding transforms passive acceptance into active, strategic problem-solving and ensures that the entire organization is deeply invested in steering the company toward its goals. TGIF proves that open-door dialogue is not a soft cultural feature, but a hard strategic imperative.

Buffer: The Protective Filter in Action

The social media management company Buffer provides a modern case study in supportive leadership. As they scaled, leaders recognized they needed to act as a filter, strategically saying "no" to distracting projects that didn't align with core goals. They also prioritized the courage of constructive accountability, addressing performance issues directly and proactively.

By moving from a reactive mindset to a defensive, proactive one, they minimized crises and created an environment where employees felt valued, protected, and thus empowered to dedicate their full energy to the company's success. This supportive approach yields famously high morale and low turnover.

Summary: Leadership as the Engine of Sustainable Growth

The engine for sustainable organizational growth isn't an external strategy or a silver-bullet technology. It is the deliberate and consistent practice of effective leadership. The reliance on hierarchy and fear fosters passive compliance and inevitably leads to disengagement, intellectual stagnation, and costly turnover.

The collaborative leadership model demands that leaders trade the limiting role of the solitary dictator for that of the Chief Enabler. This essential shift requires leveraging inquiry, authentic dialogue, and radical transparency—particularly through the method of Appreciative Inquiry—to transform organizational change from an imposed mandate into a shared mission of co-creation. This approach not only unlocks the collective potential of the team but is a direct driver of profitability and innovation.

Great leaders anticipate challenges by practicing proactive planning, and they protect their teams' focus by acting as a filter against unnecessary demands. They demonstrate courage by addressing difficult conversations directly, thereby fostering a culture of trust and accountability. Ultimately, the most effective leaders prove that true authority is rooted in influence, not title, empowering, supporting, and recognizing their teams to unlock the full potential and resilience of the entire organization.

CHAPTER 4
CREATING RESULTS TOGETHER: THE COLLABORATIVE ENGINE OF GROWTH

In the preceding chapters, we established the foundational power of collaborative leadership—a style rooted in influence, inquiry, and trust. Now, our focus shifts to the operational reality of a fully collaborative organization: the true value of a culture where results are not merely the product of individual effort, but of collective problem-solving and shared purpose. This is the crucial intersection where leadership philosophy translates directly into measurable, sustainable outcomes.

The Strategic Power of Problems

Every organization, regardless of its size or maturity, faces daily challenges. The way leaders and teams respond to these problems fundamentally shapes not only the immediate outcomes but also the company's long-term culture and collective capabilities. Effective leaders see every problem not as an obstacle, but as a catalyst for transformative growth and innovation. They understand that the nature of a problem is less important than the quality of the collaborative process used to solve it.

This vital shift requires moving away from outcome obsession, the anxiety and fixation on the result, to an intense, daily focus on mastering the necessary inputs. This mindset is best exemplified by organizations that have transformed existential threats into enduring assets.

For instance, the legendary hot dog stand in Los Angeles, Pink's Hot Dogs, faced a financial crisis when their landlord planned a substantial rent hike. This was a classic business problem, a threat to financial stability that demanded immediate reaction. Instead of merely negotiating or relocating, the owners saw the problem as an opportunity to secure their future.

They used a combination of financing and strategic resolve to buy the land their stand sat on, turning a high-risk liability into a permanent asset for the business. They did not solve the symptom (high rent); they solved the root cause (lack of ownership).

Similarly, in a different context, a Cleveland radio personality like Alan Freed did not just play music. He actively defined a cultural moment by coining the term rock and roll.

In the early 1950s, the music industry was facing the problem of changing demographics with a growing youth market whose tastes were not reflected in the existing radio formats. Freed's proactive and collaborative engagement with the music and the audience demonstrated how a clear, defining response to an evolving market can create an entirely new landscape of opportunity.

He did not resist the change. He gave it a name, unifying a disparate genre and market under a powerful, collective identity. Collaborative problem-solving in business is therefore not just about removing friction. It is about transforming the way people think and interact, building a collective capacity that is definitively greater than the sum of its individual parts.

The Discipline of Root Cause Analysis

In the business world, a solution is only truly valuable when it is robust enough to endure. The greatest operational failure is not the result of a single mistake. It is the result of the failure to learn, and this results in the repeated, costly cycle of solving the same problem over and over. The fundamental principle is clear: quick fixes don't work!

The Crisis of the Quick Fix

The intense, often daily pressure to deliver a quick fix is a familiar yet dangerous trap. Quick fixes offer a temporary illusion of relief, but they consistently create anxiety, short-circuit critical thinking, and result in surface-level solutions.

This leads directly to the exhausting game of whack-a-mole, where fixing one symptom immediately causes a related, and often more complex, problem to surface elsewhere. For example, a company might address poor customer support scores by hiring more phone agents (the quick fix). While the wait time (the immediate symptom) drops, the poor scores persist because the actual cause is a confusing product interface that generates unnecessary calls in the first place (the root cause). This cycle is the direct result of a short-term, reactive mindset that focuses on immediate pain rather than systemic causes.

Leaders often gravitate toward treating symptoms because they are the loudest, most visible pain points. This approach feels easier and faster than addressing systemic issues, which typically require significant, uncomfortable changes to core processes or culture—a path many leaders avoid by prioritizing temporary satisfaction.

Senior leaders also frequently suffer from a dual challenge of: (i) being too close to the problem, meaning they are so immersed in the daily urgency that they are unable to see the systemic patterns, and (ii) focusing on symptoms, reacting to pain instead of the root cause, akin to perpetually bailing water from a leaky boat instead of patching the hole.

Asking, "What do we do?" is a demand for a bandage. It ignores the infection underneath, and crucially, it bypasses the need for collective, deep inquiry.

From Reaction to Inquiry

To break this destructive cycle, leaders must develop the resolve to identify the underlying issue. This starts by shifting the dialogue from knee-jerk reaction to deep, collaborative inquiry.

The immediate response, "What do we do?" leads to a narrow, immediate fix that stifles creative thinking. A more powerful question is, "What if?" an invitation to discovery that engages collective intelligence and unlocks systemic thinking.

This strategic query opens the floor to systemic investigation. For example, instead of asking, "How do we fix the high error rate in our new hires by providing more training?" the collaborative leader asks, "What if the deficient onboarding process is causing the high error rate, because we aren't clarifying the performance metrics during the first week?" This ensures the focus is on finding a lasting cure for sustainable growth, not just applying a temporary patch.

The Collaborative Method: A Framework for Enduring Solutions

Effective leadership demands we become persistent detectives who move beyond symptoms to solve problems once and for all. This requires deliberate action and cultural discipline. Leaders must consciously pause before implementing immediate solutions, asking, "How long will this solution last?" rather than "How fast can we fix this?" This is a key mental shift from speed to durability.

Furthermore, they must develop a culture of inquiry by making it safe for employees to challenge assumptions using tools like the Five Whys to articulate the causal relationship of the problem.

For instance, the sales report was late. Why? Because the data was inaccurate. Why? Because the new data entry system was confusing. Why? Because the training was rushed. Why? Because the rollout schedule was compressed to meet an aggressive deadline. Why? And here we find the root cause: the leadership team prioritized a fast system launch over proper staff training.

To ensure the solution addresses the entire system, not just one silo's view, leaders must seek diverse perspectives, pulling together a cross-functional group that includes managers, frontline staff, and relevant engineers. Solutions devised in isolation are almost always suboptimal.

By involving the people who do the work every day, the team gains critical insight into operational friction points that the executive suite often misses. Finally, be prepared to invest in systemic change, committing the necessary time and capital to lasting fixes, and to prioritizing long-term solutions over short-term gains, even when those long-term solutions cause discomfort or are expensive upfront.

This method relies entirely on collective intelligence. Leaders must unify the problem statement by encouraging the entire team to ask: why? They also must ensure they all understand the core problem and agree upon desired results before jumping to solutions. They must also share the process by communicating why—why the data, the trade-offs, and the alternatives considered—to build intrinsic buy-in and disarm resistance. Including all team members in the reasoning behind changes fundamentally reduces the common resistance to change, transforming passive compliance into active ownership.

To mitigate the fear of large shifts, leaders should employ strategic change management by breaking down big changes into manageable steps, lowering the emotional barrier to adoption, and ensuring continuous, psychologically safe progress.

Consider the detailed example of the recurring customer complaints. A major software company was caught in the whack-a-mole cycle, constantly patching individual bugs reported by customers (the symptom). This meant the engineering team was perpetually exhausted and customer satisfaction metrics flatlined. Leadership decided to pause the firefighting. They formed a diverse cross-functional team, including developers, QA testers, the sales reps who had heard the complaints first-hand, and the customer support staff.

The team applied the Five Whys analysis. They realized that most bugs were being caught *after* release. Why? Because the QA process was being rushed. Why? Because of the unsustainable, aggressive development schedule imposed by management. Why? Because the sales team was pushing for faster product cycles to hit their quarterly targets. Why? And now we arrive at the root cause: a systemic misalignment between sales targets and engineering capacity planning.

The quick fix would have been to hire more QA testers, but the solution was far more robust: investing heavily in automated testing, which would allow faster testing without adding staff, and moving to longer, stable release cycles coordinated directly with sales targets.

This required a significant commitment of time and money upfront and a difficult conversation with the sales leadership, but it led to a dramatic and sustained reduction in customer complaints (by over 60% in one year), lower employee stress, and soaring customer satisfaction. This proved that investing in systemic change is the direct, most reliable path to sustainable growth.

Cross-Department Problem Solving

Collaboration must extend beyond solving single problems to become part of the entire organizational structure. True business growth demands effective collaboration across all areas, yet too many companies operate in rigid, isolated silos—a phenomenon often called parallel play, where teams work near each other but not *with* each other, optimizing for their own success at the expense of the organization's total output.

The Problem of Siloed Operations

When departments work independently, their efforts frequently cancel each other out, preventing the business from achieving true, scalable growth. Each silo is trying to maximize its own score, blind to the downstream effects on others. The most damaging symptom of this isolation is costly misalignment.

For example, in a manufacturing company, a high-performing

sales team might secure a massive order and promise a tight delivery timeline to a major client. However, because they failed to consult with the operations and supply chain teams on existing factory workload, raw material lead times, and shipping capacity, the factory simply cannot meet the deadline.

This disconnect leads to missed deadlines, costly rush orders, damaged brand credibility, and intense pressure on operational staff to somehow deliver the impossible. This is a direct threat to the bottom line caused by unaligned goals. Furthermore, sales growth often stalls, not from a lack of effort, but from a profound lack of synergy.

When leaders operate in isolation, focusing only on their own departmental metrics, the organization loses the collective power required to move beyond stagnation and compete effectively in the market. The customer experiences the company as a single entity, and siloed behavior results in a fractured, inconsistent customer experience.

The Solution: Working in Concert

The antidote is the unwavering commitment that leaders must have to work in concert, not alone. True growth requires all teams to be aligned and to function as a single, coherent system, recognizing their interdependence as a source of strength.

To achieve this cross-functional synergy, organizations must establish structured collaboration. This means facilitating regular interdepartmental meetings with a clear mandate to discuss dependencies and flag potential roadblocks *before* they become crises. This is about prevention, not reaction.

Leaders must also align goals across departments. For example, instead of judging sales solely on volume and operations solely on cost, departmental metrics should be tied to overarching organizational goals, such as linking sales targets to operations capacity. This creates a shared understanding of risk and opportunity. To build bridges, not silos, implement systems that allow departments to share updates, timelines, and capacity constraints in real time (like shared dashboards or integrated planning software). This transparency prevents one team from unknowingly creating a crisis for another.

Finally, when major challenges arise, leaders must encourage collaborative problem-solving by mandating the formation of cross-functional teams to co-create the solution, leveraging diverse perspectives and embedding the principle of shared ownership.

Take the detailed example of overpromised delivery. A consumer goods company celebrated a major sales win, securing a contract that promised a 30% jump in revenue. But, because the sales department was incentivized solely on the volume of deals closed and failed to consult with operations on capacity, they could not meet the tight deadline without disrupting all other scheduled shipments.

The result was delayed shipments for the new customer and existing clients, leading to a damaged brand reputation. The leadership responded not with blame, but with systemic change. They immediately changed the commission structure for the sales team to include a multiplier based on on-time delivery as confirmed by operations. Furthermore, they mandated weekly **Capacity Review** meetings that were interdepartmental and implemented a shared, real-time dashboard that showed factory load and inventory levels, and this dashboard was accessible by both Sales and Operations.

The outcome was that sales began checking capacity *before* promising delivery, the company consistently delivered on time, and the business grew sustainably and predictably because they were no longer hobbled by internal friction. This demonstrated that breaking down silos is a strategic necessity that protects your brand, maximizes collective power, and is the true engine that drives sustainable growth.

New Results Require New Ideas: Embracing Proactive Evolution

In a rapidly changing business environment, even the most successful strategies have a limited shelf life. Leaders cannot afford to become complacent—what worked yesterday may not work tomorrow. Long-term growth depends on a steady, continuous flow of fresh perspectives and innovative thinking, not just minor tweaks to old plans.

The Imperative for Continuous Evolution

When results stall despite strong execution, it is a clear sign that yesterday's strategies are no longer sufficient. The business world is dynamic and every initiative, no matter how effective at first, will eventually need to evolve. The most effective leaders look beyond the immediate horizon, constantly building a pipeline of new ideas and initiatives to catch the next wave of opportunity.

This process is not about discarding past success. It is about strategically building on it. Leaders must recognize that while their teams execute the decisions made, they often do not see the full range of options considered at the top.

To stay ahead, organizations always need more—and better—options than they have today. The hallmark of a proactive leader is that they are actively funding the next wave of success *before* the current wave crests.

The Danger of Strategic Complacency

The greatest threat to long-term success is not external competition but internal inertia. The most common pitfall is becoming complacent and waiting until old strategies are no longer effective before taking action. This passive stance guarantees the organization will always be operating from a position of weakness, reacting to market shifts rather than shaping them.

Leaders must recognize a fundamental truth: what worked

yesterday may not always work tomorrow, because every initiative—no matter how initially effective—will eventually become insufficient. Success breeds a temporary sense of security, but the market, customer behavior, and technology all evolve relentlessly.

If the leadership mindset remains static, the company is essentially programming itself for future decline, guaranteeing that its best thinking will always lag behind the needs of the moment. The history of business is littered with companies that executed a perfect strategy right up until the moment that strategy became obsolete.

Solutions: Proactive Strategy Development

To defeat strategic complacency and ensure continuous relevance, leaders must commit to a proactive, forward-looking discipline. This starts with cultivating new ideas. You must continuously develop new initiatives to stay ahead of the curve.

This is about making the deliberate effort to build on old ideas while aggressively seeking replacements for those that are nearing their expiration date. This means treating the strategy pipeline as a continuous development cycle, not a static annual plan.

To ensure the organization never suffers from idea scarcity, leaders must widen the flow of fresh perspectives. This requires looking beyond the usual sources of innovation—the C-suite or R&D department—and soliciting ideas from every level of the organization. A continuous flow of strategies and inviting contribution from multiple points within the organization, all allows the company to evolve with the times.

This inclusive approach empowers the entire team to sense emerging market needs and competitive threats, transforming the organization from a reactive follower into a proactive trendsetter. Innovation often comes from the perspective of the frontline worker who observes customer behavior directly, not just the executive suite.

Sustaining a competitive edge requires institutionalizing a deliberate, proactive approach to generating and testing new ideas—an innovation cycle. The first step is to institutionalize review and experimentation by regularly reviewing and updating strategies and by encouraging teams to propose and experiment with new ideas. Strategy must be a continuous process of examination and adaptation, allocating dedicated time and resources for small-scale, internal experiments.

Leaders must then widen the idea pipeline by creating structured feedback loops, cross-functional idea workshops, and transparent processes that acknowledge every valuable contribution.

Finally, effective strategy is built on evolving away from the past. Leaders must analyze what has worked before but remain flexible and be ready to allow those strategies to evolve to meet current and future needs. This requires balancing institutional knowledge with a resistance to nostalgia. Understand the principles behind past success, then ask how those principles must be radically updated to account for today's market shifts and emerging technologies.

Consider a retail chain through continuous innovation. A national retail chain enjoyed years of growth by relying on its successful strategy of offering wide product selection and competitive prices in high-traffic centers. This cemented the company as a household name.

However, as online shopping exploded and consumer preferences shifted toward convenience and personalization, the chain's sales began to stall even though store managers and staff were executing the existing strategy flawlessly. This was the blindness of past success; their strategy was becoming obsolete. Leadership initially doubled down on traditional promotions, but results continued to lag.

Recognizing the urgent need for fresh perspectives, the CEO launched a company-wide initiative to gather new ideas from all levels. Employees from sales associates to warehouse staff were invited to share insights. The company also formed cross-functional teams to quickly begin to experiment with new concepts such as in-store pickup for online orders, personalized shopping experiences, and community-focused events.

Instead of discarding its foundational strengths, the company strategically built on them by leveraging trusted customer service and convenient locations, all while adapting to new digital trends. They piloted a loyalty app, completely revamped their website, and reimagined store layouts to seamlessly blend digital and physical shopping.

As a result, the retail chain not only reversed its sales decline but also fostered a vibrant culture of innovation and ownership. By proactively seeking new ideas and maintaining strategic flexibility, the company ensured its long-term growth and relevance.

Creating Opportunity From Failure

Not every new idea will succeed and that is perfectly okay. In fact, some of the most valuable lessons come from setbacks and failures, especially when organizations seek feedback from multiple perspectives. While personal and professional milestones are worth celebrating, it is often the moments when we fall short that leave the deepest, most lasting impact.

The Wisdom in Loss

The excitement of achievement can be fleeting, but the insights gained from *not* reaching a goal often become the bedrock for future success. Failure is not something to dismiss. It is a source of invaluable wisdom and motivation. It pushes us to dig deeper, ask tough questions, and collectively confront what truly went wrong.

Winning feels great, and success certainly leaves clues. But the most powerful lessons are not found in victory laps. They are discovered in the aftermath of a loss. The sting of failure lingers, serving as a powerful motivator to improve, innovate, and adapt. By auditing our losses instead of just celebrating our wins, we uncover hidden weaknesses and opportunities for growth that success alone could never reveal.

This insight, that we learn more from our losses than from our wins, is counterintuitive. Wins confirm our current method, but losses force us to question the underlying assumptions and systems.

The problem with fearing missteps is that by dismissing failures you fail to gain wisdom. When leaders and teams are conditioned to view failure as an endpoint—a source of blame or embarrassment—they cover it up, ignore it, or move past it as quickly as possible.

This reaction is a critical loss as the detailed data contained within a setback is often far more revealing than the data contained within a success. This leads directly to the complementary problem of only learning from wins.

While celebrating achievements builds morale, relying solely on victories for strategic insight can make an organization strategically blind. Wins confirm your existing methods, providing no pressure to question assumptions or seek new approaches. By contrast, a loss provides a mandatory stress test of your systems, your communication, and your strategy.

Solutions: The Discipline of Auditing Loss

To successfully convert failure into fuel for future growth, leaders must institutionalize a discipline of strategic review. The solution is simple yet non-negotiable: audit and learn from your losses.

This requires leadership to review setbacks, failures, and missed goals to uncover valuable lessons and opportunities for improvement. Instead of shying away from uncomfortable results, a collaborative culture treats every shortfall as a mandatory research project.

This process, often formalized as an After-Action Review (AAR), moves beyond surface-level critiques such as "The sales team missed the quota," to asking systemic, causal questions. Why was the training insufficient? Why did our capacity estimation fail? By rigorously analyzing the failure points in a non-judgmental environment, the organization extracts the specific, actionable intelligence that reveals hidden weaknesses, allowing teams to build stronger systems and more robust strategies for the next attempt.

The action needed for this transformation is clear: formalize the failure review by treating every missed goal or failed project as a mandatory research assignment. The AAR must be collaborative and systemic, involving all relevant stakeholders, and must establish psychological safety as its non-negotiable foundation.

Once the lessons are extracted, they must be permanently embedded into the organizational DNA. Leaders must integrate lessons learned from failures into future strategies. This requires specific, measurable changes to core processes, training modules, or strategic frameworks. If a failed product launch was due to poor cross-functional communication, the lesson must be integrated by creating new mandatory interdepartmental meetings. The organization should never be allowed to make the same high-cost mistake twice.

A powerful illustration is found in auditing losses to drive innovation at a retail chain. The chain launched a new loyalty app, expecting it to boost sales. After several months, adoption rates were low, and customer feedback was mixed. The initial reaction was disappointment, and suggestions arose to quietly shelve the project—the classic mistake of dismissing failure.

Instead, the company chose to treat this setback as a learning opportunity. They scheduled structured review sessions with cross-functional teams—marketing, IT, store managers, and customer service—to openly discuss what went wrong. Critically, employees were encouraged to share honest feedback without fear of blame.

Through these discussions, several key systemic issues surfaced. For one, the app's interface was confusing. Second, store staff hadn't been properly trained to promote it. And, most importantly, customers wanted more personalized rewards, rewards the app did not offer.

The company documented these hard-won lessons and shared them across departments. Rather than abandoning the initiative, leadership integrated the feedback into a revised app strategy. They simplified the user experience, launched dedicated staff training programs, and redesigned the rewards system based directly on customer input. Progress was tracked, and changes were continually refined.

Within a year, the loyalty app became one of the chain's most successful digital tools, driving increased sales and customer satisfaction. By auditing their losses and learning from failure, the company turned an initial setback into a foundation for future success, proving that failure is an asset when intentionally studied and collaboratively addressed.

Case Study: BrightPath Solutions

Imagine a mid-sized software startup, BrightPath Solutions, that specializes in workflow automation tools for small businesses. After a promising launch, the company hit a wall. Customer complaints about bugs were rising, support tickets were piling up, and new feature releases were consistently delayed. Morale was low, and the leadership team was under pressure to deliver quick fixes.

The Quick Fix Trap. Initially, BrightPath's leaders responded by hiring more customer support agents and pushing developers to work overtime. This temporarily reduced wait times, but customer satisfaction scores remained flat. The real problem persisted as the product itself was confusing, and bugs kept slipping through the cracks. The company was stuck in a cycle of whack-a-mole, treating symptoms instead of root causes.

The Shift to Collaborative Problem-Solving. Recognizing the futility of quick fixes, the CEO called for a company-wide pause. Instead of another round of reactive measures, BrightPath formed a cross-functional task force consisting of developers, QA testers, support agents, sales reps, and even a few customers were invited to participate.

Applying Root Cause Analysis. Using the **Five Whys** method, the team traced the recurring bugs back to a rushed QA process. Why was QA rushed? Because the release schedule was too aggressive. Why was the schedule so tight? Because sales targets demanded frequent launches. Why were sales targets set this way? Because leadership hadn't aligned sales goals with engineering capacity. The root cause was a systemic misalignment between departments.

Building Cross-Department Synergy. Armed with these insights, BrightPath's leaders restructured their approach. This included:

- **Weekly Capacity Review Meetings.** Sales, engineering, and support met regularly to discuss upcoming releases, capacity constraints, and customer feedback.
- **Shared Dashboards.** Real-time data on product status, support trends, and sales forecasts were made accessible to all teams.
- **Aligned Incentives.** Sales commissions were now tied to on-time delivery and customer satisfaction, not just deal volume.

Embracing Proactive Evolution. BrightPath did not stop at fixing the immediate problem. Leadership launched an Innovation Pipeline initiative, inviting ideas from every level of the company. Frontline support agents suggested a new onboarding wizard to reduce confusion for new users. Developers proposed automated testing tools to catch bugs earlier. These ideas were piloted, refined, and—when successful—scaled across the company.

Auditing Losses and Learning from Failure. Not every experiment worked. A new feature aimed at enterprise clients flopped, leading to disappointing sales. Instead of hiding the failure, BrightPath held an After-Action Review (AAR), inviting honest feedback from all stakeholders. They discovered the feature was poorly marketed and didn't address actual customer pain points. Lessons learned were documented and shared, leading to a revamped product strategy that better matched customer needs.

Summary: Sustainable Solutions Through Collaborative Internal Inquiry

In this chapter, we explored how both powerful solutions and sustainable growth come from within; that is, by harnessing the collective wisdom, experience, and creativity already present in your organization. The answers to your toughest challenges aren't outside consultants or quick fixes; they're in the building, waiting to be discovered through intentional collaboration and a commitment to looking inward.

Creating lasting results requires an intentional focus on five key pillars of collaborative action. First, organizations must adopt the **Discipline of Root Cause Analysis**, addressing the source of problems rather than just the symptoms. This means resisting the quick fix and instead fostering a culture of deep inquiry that seeks diverse perspectives to drive systemic, enduring change, effectively ending the exhausting game of whack-a-mole.

Second, leaders must empower the entire team, recognizing that the best solutions come from collective intelligence, not isolated expertise. This is achieved by clarifying problems, communicating the *why* behind changes, and actively soliciting contributions from all levels. This prevents blind spots and builds trust.

The remaining pillars focus on maximizing organizational potential for sustainable growth. To eliminate internal friction, leaders must break down silos and end parallel play by aligning departmental goals and mandating cross-functional communication, ensuring teams work in concert to reliably deliver on promises.

Simultaneously, the organization must embrace the proactive and fight complacency by treating strategy as a continuous innovation cycle. This means constantly inviting fresh perspectives and developing new initiatives because even the best past strategies have a limited shelf life.

Finally, and most critically, organizations must audit their losses. Instead of fearing failure, leaders must institutionalize the After-Action Review process to collaboratively study shortfalls,

The collaborative leader's final responsibility is to create an environment where these five pillars are not just practiced but institutionalized, transforming the organization from one that simply reacts to challenges into one that strategically evolves through collective intelligence.

CHAPTER 5
RESIST SCALING FROM THE OUTSIDE

In the pursuit of organizational growth, leaders often find themselves chasing the innovations of competitors, attending every major industry event, and relentlessly seeking public acclaim or media validation.

This outward focus, while intuitive, is ultimately a distraction. The truth this chapter seeks to uncover is that true and sustainable progress begins within. We invite leaders to fundamentally shift their perspective from external benchmarks to internal strengths, recognizing that the enduring power of a healthy culture and authentic employee support are the only genuine engines of organizational growth.

This principle demands a new view of your offering. Forget the safety net of relying solely on standard product offerings; instead, consider the transformative potential of custom work. By committing your expertise to solve unique, messy challenges for clients, the problems that off-the-shelf solutions simply can't touch—you build profound trust, deepen relationships, and become truly indispensable. This unique approach opens the door to fulfilling all a client's evolving needs, cementing the kind of long-term partnerships that secure a business for the future.

Growth starts not with a market analysis, but with a deceptively simple, yet profound, question: Who buys our stuff? The honest, strategic answer to this query forms the bedrock of your entire strategy, guiding exactly how you reach, serve, and retain your customers. Rather than chasing the competition or reacting to industry noise, the strategic priority is to understand and serve the customers you already have.

This internal focus empowers you to refine your channels, nurture loyalty, expand your offerings organically, and, most importantly, simplify your customers' experience. Resisting the reflexive pressure to scale through purely external, attention-seeking means—like generic industry trade shows or media spotlights—frees up crucial resources. It allows you to invest in genuine connections, whether that's attending intimate customer conferences, listening deeply to internal employee feedback, or building a professional network based on generosity and unwavering trust.

The most meaningful rewards of leadership are ultimately found not in fleeting public acclaim, but in the sustained voices of those you support and inspire. This chapter, therefore, explores a simple but powerful thesis: looking inward is the most reliable path to driving upward growth, making your organization not just bigger, but demonstrably better.

The Gold Standard of Growth: Inward Focus, Outward Impact

Scaling an organization from the outside in leads to brittle, short-lived results, leaving the company fragile and vulnerable to external shocks. Sustainable growth—the kind that makes you better, not just bigger—is based on a few basic, unchanging rules that force you to focus on your lasting internal strengths instead of distracting outside noise..

The simple question, "Who buys our stuff?" is merely the starting

RESIST SCALING FROM THE OUTSIDE

point; the answer requires identifying your target client with surgical precision. Growth is never about expanding into every possible market. It is about deepening your value to the *right* people.

When you know exactly who you serve best, you gain clarity on where to invest your resources and which relationships to prioritize. This clarity acts as a powerful strategic filter, allowing you to confidently resist chasing growth opportunities that distract you from your key strengths.

This focus on the right client directly enables the next principle: do not sell products, give unique solutions to problems. While standardized products provide operational stability, transformative growth comes from custom products and/or services.

Your most valuable clients are struggling with unique, messy, human-system problems that packaged, off-the-shelf solutions cannot solve. By using your deft hand to navigate and solve these complex challenges, you elevate the relationship beyond a transaction and provide a customized architectural solution that makes your clients' organizations fundamentally better.

This commitment to unique problem-solving is how you become truly indispensable and cement the deep trust required for a profitable, long-term partnership. The proof of this commitment is your most valuable asset. Cherish the authentic words of your clients, whose testimonials become the irrefutable proof of your unique value proposition in action.

This internal, client-centric focus naturally shifts the entire orientation of the business. Your focus should be on your customers, not your competition. Competitor-centric strategy leads only to mimicry and a frantic, undignified race to the bottom on price.

The only benchmark that truly matters is whether you are delivering increasing value as well as simplifying the experience for the people who have chosen you. Prioritize their needs, listen to their evolving challenges, and make their success your core measure of victory.

This philosophy extends even to professional engagement; true networking is a mindset—it is what you give, not what you get.

Building a professional network based on generosity and trust is the only way to ensure the relationships that ultimately drive your growth will naturally emerge. And you can do this all without succumbing to the transactional exchange of hunting for leads.

Finally, the best feedback for a leader comes from inside their company or organization. The most meaningful rewards of leadership are found not in public acclaim, but in the voices of those you support and inspire. A leader must seek out employee feedback as the clearest, most honest view of the organization's health.

The Traps of External Validation

The path to scaling from within requires immense discipline. This is because the corporate world is engineered to constantly pull you outward, manifesting in predictable traps that derail even the most well-intentioned leaders.

Perhaps the most common trap is the Fear of Missing Out (FOMO), a crippling preoccupation with the competition. This fear is a massive tax on strategic thinking, leading leaders to invest in every buzzword technology and to mimic every new feature launched by a rival.

This creates a cluttered, inconsistent strategy that satisfies no one. To build something truly lasting, a leader must resist the anxiety that can arise when watching the competition. Instead, they must commit fully to the unique value only they can provide to their target client.

The second major trap is transactional networking—the shallow belief that professional connection is about what you can get, not what you can give. Transactional networking views every meeting as a chance to pitch, fundamentally poisoning the well of long-term opportunity and failing to build the genuine alliances that pay dividends for the entire life of your business.

Finally, there is the trap of chasing the spotlight. This is where leaders seek public applause, becoming addicted to validation in media mentions and vanity metrics. This hunger for external recognition is a distraction from the quiet, difficult work of building a healthy internal culture.

A leader focused on the spotlight is rarely focused on the messy details of the complex human system that runs the business, resulting in a fragile organization that looks good on the cover of a magazine but that is hollow on the inside.

Building from the Inside Out

The antidote to external anxiety, transactional thinking, and the pursuit of fleeting spotlights is simple: recommit your focus to the interior of your organization. Shifting your priorities from chasing public validation to achieving private excellence is the most strategic and disciplined move a leader can make.

The solution to the competitor trap is to simply look away. Your single-minded imperative should be to focus on your customers—to listen deeply, simplify their experience, and anticipate their needs.

When you make your customers your obsession, you naturally leapfrog the competition. The antidote to transactional networking is authenticity, that is, approaching networking with the consideration of what you can give. When you lead with generosity and offer value without asking for a return, you establish trust, and trust is the currency of sustainable relationships.

To counter the pursuit of external acclaim, leaders must embrace the real ego trip, which comes from the voices within their own organization and the candid opinions of their employees. Your true validation as a leader lies in the health of your internal human system where a thriving, resilient culture becomes a permanent competitive advantage.

From Theory to Internal Strength

The commitment to scaling from the inside out requires specific, systematic action. These steps serve as the practical application of using a deft hand to manage the human system, ensuring that the theory of *The Answers Are in the Building* becomes a reliable foundation for real-world results.

Pinpoint Your Target

To shift from chasing low-margin volume to achieving strategic, profitable growth, you must first create an *Anti-Client Profile* that defines the type of client you will refuse to take. This negative clarity filters out time-wasting work.

Next, audit your best clients by reviewing your top successful client engagements, and then create a precise target profile based on genuine data, not external benchmarks. Use this analysis to build detailed client personas that reflect not just demographics, but their unique human-system pain points, which then serve as the narrative guide for your entire organization.

Finally, adjust your channels by directing all marketing and sales efforts *only* toward the places where your target client spends their time.

Commit to Customization

To shift your offering from a commodity to an essential partnership, institute a *Discovery Gap Protocol.* This is where your team must uncover at least three unique, non-obvious pain points *before* presenting a standard product. If you cannot find a unique problem, you cannot offer a unique solution.

Then, take the **Customization Challenge.** Pitch at least one highly customized component that directly addresses a unique pain point to demonstrate your commitment to a specific solution.

You must carefully record the client's situation before and after your service to clearly show the unique value of your expert guidance, turning those stories into powerful sales materials. This process must be institutionalized through deep client engagement and by training your team for creativity, empowering them to prioritize problem-solving over standard sales pitches.

Validate from Within

To make the voices of your customers and employees your primary benchmark, you must first set up regular channels for collecting feedback such as anonymous surveys to make providing honest insight safe and routine.

Practice active listening and implement changes based on this feedback, recognizing that action reinforces integrity. Establish a **Retention Loop** by asking your longest-retained clients, "What is the one thing we do that our competitors could never copy?" Their answer will give you a permanent advantage.

Finally, ignore heading to the **Industry Trade Show**. Reallocate that budget to hosting small, exclusive meetings of customer advisory boards. From these meetings you will gain high-value, specific feedback that drives actual improvement.

Build Trust Capital

To redefine your professional interactions as opportunities for generosity, commit to the *Introduction Challenge*. In this challenge you make one meaningful, unsolicited introduction per week without asking for anything in return.

Offer the *Perspective Offer*. This is when you provide candid, high-value advice to a peer without charging or hinting at future engagement. This demonstrates your intention to lead with help and knowledge and build genuine relationships.

Ultimately, measure *Trust Capital, Not Leads* by shifting your internal reporting to track meaningful connections that you have assisted. Follow up with contacts to support, not sell, building a bridge based on trust rather than burning it with a transactional pitch.

The Enduring Value of Internal Focus

Understanding the *Why* transforms these actions from mere tasks into a deeply embedded strategic philosophy. The reward for resisting external pressures and embracing the complex human system is an organization that is stronger, more trustworthy, and ultimately, indispensable to its clients.

This laser-like focus on knowing your target client ensures your growth strategies are effective and serves as the antidote to the paralyzing effect of FOMO. It allows you to allocate resources efficiently and tailor your offerings to those most likely to benefit. This is the most reliable path to profitable scaling. The commitment to unique solutions builds deeper trust and long-term relationships, making you indispensable and ensuring your competitive advantage is built on relationship quality, not price.

The feedback you receive from those you serve and work with is more valuable than public acclaim. Honest, candid feedback from employees and customers drives meaningful improvements that last. This continuous loop strengthens your culture, creates psychological safety for employees, and ensures your business remains relevant and responsive, building resilience from the inside out.

Finally, approaching networking to give to others builds trust and a strong reputation, which organically attracts opportunities. This mindset shifts your focus from competition to collaboration, fostering a resilient network where success is shared, and opportunities come to you because of the value you put out into the world.

This commitment to internal strength is what sets truly exceptional leaders apart. By mastering the human system within your organization, you stop chasing success and start *generating* it.

Case Study: CustomTech Solutions – The Power of the Inside Game

Several years before the pivotal transformation, CustomTech Solutions, known for its robust workflow automation tools tailored to healthcare providers, was a rising star in the B2B software space. The company's early success was built on technical excellence and on a knack for responding quickly to market trends. However, as the industry matured, the leadership team—like many in their position—began to feel the pressure of rapid change and fierce competition.

The Drift Toward External Focus. Industry conferences became a regular fixture on the calendar. The sales team tracked every move of their largest competitors. As well, product roadmaps were increasingly shaped by what the competition was doing. The company's marketing shifted toward broad, generic messaging in an attempt to capture a wider audience. Internally, employees felt the strain of constant pivots and shifting priorities, and the company's once-clear identity began to blur.

This outside-in approach led to short-term wins but mounting long-term challenges. Sales grew longer, customer satisfaction scores plateaued, and the team felt reactive rather than proactive. The leadership, led by CEO Maria Gotsch, realized that chasing external validation—industry awards, media mentions, and the latest buzzwords—was not translating into sustainable growth or a stronger company.

The Turning Point. Looking inward and recognizing the need for a reset, Maria called a leadership retreat. The agenda was simple: stop talking about competitors and start talking about customers. The team revisited the fundamental question: "Who buys our stuff, and why?" Through honest analysis, they discovered that their most loyal and profitable clients were not the large hospital systems they had been targeting, but rather small clinics with unique operational challenges—especially around scheduling and billing.

This insight was a revelation. Instead of spreading themselves thin,

Maria and the team decided to double down on serving this core group. They interviewed clinic managers, shadowed front-desk staff, and mapped out the daily frustrations these clients faced. This process of building detailed client personas was more than a marketing exercise, it became the company's strategic filter, helping them tune out industry noise and focus on what truly mattered.

From Commodity to Custom Partner. With a clear target in mind, Maria challenged the product team to move beyond standard offerings. She instituted what she called a listening tour, sending developers and support staff directly into clinics to hear firsthand about the obstacles staff faced—especially the burden of insurance paperwork and the complexity of patient reminders.

Inspired by these stories, the team developed a custom module that automated insurance integration and personalized patient communications. This wasn't just a new feature; it was a tailored solution that addressed pain points no competitor had bothered to understand. By solving these unique problems, CustomTech Solutions became more than a vendor—they became a trusted partner, indispensable to their clients' daily operations.

Validation from Within. As the new solution rolled out, Maria shifted the company's definition of success. Instead of chasing public recognition, she prioritized internal validation. Quarterly feedback sessions were established, inviting both clients and employees to share candid insights. When a clinic director sent a heartfelt thank-you note about reduced staff overtime, Maria celebrated the story company-wide. These moments of genuine impact became the authentic ego trip—proof that the company's inward focus was making a tangible difference.

Building Trust Capital. Networking, too, was reimagined. Rather than treating industry events as a numbers game, Maria encouraged the team to lead with generosity. They hosted free workshops for clinic administrators, shared best practices, and made introductions between clients and other trusted vendors. Follow-ups were about offering support, not making a sale. Over time, this approach built deep trust and a reputation for integrity. Referrals increased, partnerships deepened, and growth became a natural byproduct of the company's commitment to authentic relationships.

The Results. By looking inward—focusing on their people, their culture, and the real needs of their best customers—CustomTech Solutions didn't just grow bigger; they grew better. The company's journey illustrates this chapter's key message: sustainable success is built on authenticity, internal strength, and meaningful relationships, not on chasing external validation or fleeting trends.

Summary: Resisting FOMO and Scaling from the Inside Out

In the journey of organizational growth, it is overwhelmingly tempting for leaders to look outward by chasing competitors, attending every industry event, and seeking validation from the outside world. Yet, as this chapter has revealed, the most meaningful and sustainable progress begins within.

We have urged leaders to resist the pressure to scale by external measures and instead turn their attention to the heart of their organization, to its people, its culture, and its customers.

The journey begins with the question "Who buys our stuff?" This becomes the foundation for all strategies. By resisting the crowd and digging deep to create detailed client personas, organizations gain the clarity needed to tailor their offerings, build loyalty, and filter out the debilitating effects of FOMO.

True growth is not just about transactions; it's about the application of a deft hand to solve problems in unique ways. We demonstrated how custom solutions transform relationships and make a business truly indispensable.

Validation, too, is reframed. Leaders are urged to value the voices within their own organization above public acclaim. The candid opinions of employees and the heartfelt words of clients become the true measure of success. By establishing and acting upon regular feedback channels, organizations strengthen their human system and ensure they remain relevant and responsive.

We reimagined networking as an act of generosity, encouraging leaders to approach every connection with the intention to give. This powerful shift from competition to collaboration fosters a resilient network that supports sustainable growth.

This chapter's concepts echo the book's central theme that real leadership and lasting success are built on authenticity, internal strength, and meaningful relationships. By resisting the urge to scale from the outside and by investing in what matters most within, organizations do not just grow bigger. They grow better.

CHAPTER 6
FOSTERING A POSITIVE CULTURE

In this chapter, as we move deeper into the journey of organizational transformation, we will shift the focus from individual leadership to the collective heartbeat of your business: its culture.

Culture is not a mere backdrop for your strategy. It is the operating system that determines whether your strategy succeeds or fails. A brilliant strategy executed by a toxic, fearful culture will fail every time. Conversely, an average strategy executed by a culture rooted in trust, clarity, and collaboration can achieve extraordinary results.

The true answers to scaling upward aren't found in external fixes, flashy consultants, or a new brand identity. They're rooted in the everyday actions and attitudes within your walls. This chapter is fundamentally about looking inward, challenging leaders to recognize that building a positive culture is not a task to delegate to HR or an intern, but a personal responsibility to embrace and model every single day. The culture of an organization is simply the shadow cast by its leadership. If the shadow is toxic, the leadership is toxic.

The Cultural Blueprint: From Architect to Gardener

Many organizations fall into the trap of viewing culture as a static blueprint. They treat it as a broken engine you can simply swap out for a new model, believing a rebrand or a new mission statement will magically spark change.

Leaders often act as *Culture Architects*, spending months crafting a grand, one-time overhaul. They focus on structural fixes—new reporting lines, updated dress codes, or expensive off-sites—all external attempts to solve an internal problem.

Lasting transformation doesn't come from a static plan. It grows from daily, consistent habits. Culture is a living system, an organic entity shaped by every email, every meeting, every casual conversation, and, most importantly, every consequence.

The most effective leaders, conversely, are *Culture Gardeners*. They know that real change is not an act of mass construction but a continuous process of small, deliberate interventions. Their work involves the patient, strategic labor of pruning the toxic behaviors and policies that hold teams back, while tirelessly nurturing the seeds of collaboration, accountability, and trust.

A thriving culture, meticulously cultivated, is one that consistently provides four vital elements—elements that must be present in every interaction to guarantee growth.

1. **Trust.** Believing in people's capabilities and good intent. This is the fertilizer for innovation.
2. **Clarity.** Providing direction and purpose for the work, not just a list of duties. Clarity reduces anxiety and focuses effort.
3. **Support.** Offering necessary resources, training, and removing systemic roadblocks. Support signals that leadership is committed to the success of its people.
4. **Recognition.** Consistently celebrating effort, courage, and

impact, large and small. Recognition reinforces the positive behaviors that you want to see replicated.

Policies: The Silent Architects of Culture

Before the first seed of collaboration can be planted, leaders must examine the soil they are working with, particularly the written and unwritten rules that govern behavior. Every leader must ask a crucial, introspective question: "Do our policies build people up or tear them down?"

The answer reveals the true health of your organization. Policies can either empower teams and foster trust, or they can silently erode morale and stifle innovation by communicating suspicion.

Take a close look at your company's rules and routines—from expense report requirements to vacation approval processes. Are they designed to enable your people to do their best work, or are they rooted in control and a lack of trust? The difference is everything.

When policies are built from a place of trust, they act as a scaffolding for success, giving people defined structures to safely climb higher and take strategic risks. When they are built on fear designed to manage the bottom five percent of untrustworthy employees, they become cages for the productive ninety-five percent. They stifle the vast majority's potential, slowing down processes, and communicating a profound institutional distrust.

The Language of Transformation is Behavior. Dysfunction in culture is often the silent cause of persistent business problems, manifesting as high turnover, siloed teams, and stalled innovation. This dysfunction cannot be fixed with gimmicks or top-down mandates.

The foundation of a healthy culture is built from sustainable growth, improved efficiency, and true innovation. Culture isn't simply built. It's brewed through consistent, intentional action, and leaders must model the behaviors they wish to see before ever demanding them from others. They must go first.

A Trusting Environment: The Antidote to Toxicity

Trust is not merely a desirable quality. It is the cornerstone of every thriving organization and the most powerful antidote to a toxic culture. In today's high-pressure business landscape, high-performing teams don't flourish under constant oversight, micromanagement, or relentless pressure. They thrive when given space, autonomy, and the freedom to be authentic.

This psychological safety is not a luxury or a soft skill. It is the prerequisite for high performance—the bedrock of every healthy, growing company. Without safety, no one will take the risk required to innovate.

The Tug-of-War: Control vs. Contribution

Every organization is perpetually engaged in a constant tug-of-war for its very soul. We can see this as toxicity versus inspiration. The outcome of this battle for cultural control depends entirely on leadership's daily, moment-to-moment choices. Servant leaders understand that maintaining a healthy culture takes extraordinary discipline and attentiveness, and they prioritize creating environments where teams are motivated to pursue something bigger than themselves—a shared purpose—rather than just avoiding punishment.

The Hidden Costs. The most damaging trend we observe in some struggling businesses is that leaders are limiting opportunity and manipulating their people rather than motivating and inspiring them. This focus on rigid control signals a deep-seated lack of trust, which suffocates the business.

When leadership's default posture is suspicion—when the goal is to manage the bottom five percent of perceived slackers—the organization's potential is capped, and its best talent eventually leaves. A focus on control limits growth; a focus on contribution unlocks it.

A culture of trust is built on three pillars of leader behavior—pillars that must be consciously reinforced through:

1. **Empowerment.** Ensuring employees have a voice in decision-making, and influence is not reserved only for those at the top. This means truly valuing the opinion of the person closest to the customer or the product.
2. **Support.** Equipping teams with the necessary tools, resources, and clarity to succeed. Leaders must view their role as removing roadblocks, not creating new ones.
3. **Freedom to Fail.** Allowing team members the discretion to truly lead, to experiment, and to learn from mistakes without fear of immediate repercussion. This converts error into learning capital.

Conflict as a Catalyst for Growth

Workplace conflict is not just inevitable—it is a sign of engagement. If you have passionate, smart people working toward a common goal, they will disagree. The conflict itself is rarely just about the issue at hand. It's often an emotionally charged situation—a reflection of deeper anxieties about respect, fairness, or stability that have been allowed to fester.

In these intense moments, the leader's response is the deciding factor, capable of either escalating tension into a full-blown crisis or resolving it by modeling empathy and curiosity.

It is critical to shift our perception. Conflict isn't a red flag—it's a sign that your team cares enough to fight for the best possible outcome. The true challenge for high-performing teams isn't avoiding conflict altogether, as that would mean avoiding passion and strong ideas. The result is stagnation.

The challenge is navigating it without breaking trust. When a culture lacks this foundational trust, every disagreement becomes a personal attack. The strongest cultures are instead built on the courage to face reality and repair relationships after disagreements, strengthening the bonds in the process.

To truly excel, your high-performing team needs space, not pressure. This generous space allows profound trust to take root. It is the mechanism that transforms conflict—which is inevitable in a passionate workplace—from a destructive, dividing force into a catalyst for growth and deeper understanding. The lesson here is that you must provide psychological space where employees feel safe to fail and where they have an emotional space to disagree.

The Leader's Toolkit: Cultivating Solutions

Defeating toxicity and enabling growth requires more than just good intentions. It demands awareness, true accountability, deep empathy, genuine empowerment, and consistent recognition. The solution lies in leaders committing to a set of disciplines that shift the culture from one of fear to one of competence and contribution.

The following five action steps, paired with their rationale and execution methods, represent the practice required to build and sustain a trusting environment.

1. Model Vulnerability and Authenticity

Vulnerability is the engine of trust. When leaders commit to showing vulnerability, they signal it is safe for others to do the same. This breaks down organizational barriers, reduces the fear of retribution, and makes it easier for teams to navigate conflict and innovate without the paralyzing weight of pressure.

The leader must be willing to dismantle the façade of infallibility. This starts with regularly sharing your own challenges and mistakes in team meetings, humanizing the leadership role.

Encourage open dialogue by asking for feedback. Do this by, not just by soliciting it, but by truly listening without defensiveness. The most powerful act of all is simply to admit when you do not have all the answers, inviting collective problem-solving rather than demanding blind compliance.

2. Empower Decision-Making at All Levels

Empowerment combats toxicity. This is done by shifting control from rigid hierarchy to fluid collaboration. When employees have the necessary space and authority to lead and make decisions, they feel genuinely valued, which is what truly drives high performance and engagement.

Empowerment is precise. It means you must deliberately delegate meaningful responsibilities and allow employees to make decisions within their defined roles. Set clear, explicit boundaries for autonomy so teams know where their authority begins and ends, but then—crucially—avoid micromanaging the execution. When things do not go perfectly, celebrate the initiative and the learning derived from the mistake, reinforcing that risk is a pathway to growth.

3. Create Safe Spaces for Honest Conversation

A safe environment for dialogue is essential for a healthy culture. It prevents minor issues from festering and escalating into major crises. More importantly, it allows for the essential repair of relationships after disagreements, ensuring that workplace conflict consistently leads to growth, not division.

Build safe platforms for truth. This involves establishing regular forums, such as town halls or anonymous surveys for employees to safely voice concerns and ideas. A true safe space requires leadership to respond constructively to feedback, even and especially when it is critical. Managers must be rigorously trained in conflict resolution and active listening; they are the frontline stewards of psychological safety.

4. Recognize and Celebrate Contributions

Recognition reinforces trust and motivation. It fundamentally shifts the organizational culture from one of manipulation and limitation to one of inspiration and opportunity, helping teams thrive even during challenging times.

Recognition is the fuel of motivation. Implement systems for peer-to-peer recognition alongside public acknowledgment from leadership. Recognition must be specific, timely, and tied directly to company values and positive behaviors. Publicly acknowledge both effort and impact, not just final results. This will ensure that the hard work behind the scenes is seen.

5. Embrace and Leverage Differences

Diversity is a strength, not a weakness. Embracing differences fosters deeper collaboration, boosts creativity, and builds organizational resilience. This focus ensures that your culture is built on the courage to face reality, guaranteeing that differences are leveraged to move forward, rather than causing trust to break down.

Commit to leveraging diversity. Encourage teams to seek out and integrate diverse perspectives in decision-making. By challenging black-and-white thinking and exploring multiple solutions, you convert friction into sources of powerful innovation.

Case Study: Cultural Repair in Action

The transformation at Willowbrook Medical Center, a mid-sized hospital, illustrates the immense, practical power of these principles. Facing high staff turnover and low morale, newly appointed COO Dr. Elaine Foster realized the cause was a culture of institutional mistrust and fear.

Modeling the Change. Dr. Foster began by modeling vulnerability and authenticity, openly admitting her anxieties about the new role and inviting staff to share concerns without judgment, immediately changing the power dynamic.

Empowering the Frontline. She delegated critical patient care decisions to frontline nurses, allowing them to make choices without layers of bureaucratic approval. Crucially, when new protocols were piloted, mistakes were intentionally treated as learning opportunities rather than grounds for punishment, cementing a safe environment.

Safe Spaces & Recognition. She established regular *listening rounds* and launched a peer-nominated Willowbrook Way award to publicly celebrate the small, everyday acts of kindness and teamwork. Every piece of anonymous feedback received a thoughtful, non-defensive response.

The Power of Difference. She championed the value of diverse perspectives, encouraging staff to explore multiple solutions during disagreements, and appreciating the unique strengths each person brought to the table.

The Result. Staff felt safe to speak up and take initiative. Patient satisfaction scores climbed, turnover dropped, and the hospital became known for its positive, collaborative spirit. The answers, as Dr. Foster proved, had been in the building all along—they just needed the courage and trust to surface them.

A Balanced Environment: The Key to Sustainable Excellence

A culture built on trust must also be built on the principle of sustainability. In the pursuit of a healthy workplace, balance is not an option; it is a necessity.

The most effective organizations find equilibrium. They know that when balance is missing, teams are caught in a cycle of overwhelming multitasking where anxiety rises, frustration builds, and ultimately, little is truly accomplished.

The Vicious Cycle of Control and Burnout

Despite all the talk of high performance, many organizations remain trapped in a self-defeating cycle that is fueled by outdated assumptions held by leadership. The problem is not a lack of effort but a leadership that focuses on controlling people rather than inspiring them. This controlling posture creates yes-men who are focused on job preservation, not innovation.

This is compounded by the deeply flawed belief that self-sacrifice is commitment. Leaders reward exhaustion and punish boundaries, mistakenly viewing burnout as a measure of loyalty. The result is a workforce paralyzed by overwhelming expectations. When teams are pushed to juggle too many priorities at once, anxiety soars and, despite immense effort, little is truly completed. This is the hidden cost of a control culture—it wastes energy, stifles breakthrough ideas, and guarantees failure to reach potential.

The Path to Sustainable Influence

The antidote to this vicious cycle is to create a leadership style centered on influence and on respect for human limits. Effective leaders don't control. They inspire and influence employees. They give their teams the psychological safety to contribute their best ideas, knowing that innovation cannot coexist with fear.

We must redefine commitment itself. True organizational strength does not come from self-destruction. True loyalty is not about being on the job 24/7; it is about showing up consistently and showing resilience. The only way to build a high-performance culture that lasts is to reward people for consistent, real results, not for simply working long hours or being visibly exhausted.

To achieve this, leaders must shift their focus from quantity to quality. They must empower teams to concentrate on fewer, high-impact tasks (e.g., designing and validating a new customer onboarding workflow that is projected to reduce client churn by 15%) to not only lower stress but dramatically improve outcomes. This requires the leader to be the **Chief Prioritizer,** protecting their teams from the noise of competing goals.

Finally, balance must become an institutional value. Work-life balance is a shared responsibility. The employer must create an environment where balance is encouraged and supported through policy and practice, not just lip service. Simultaneously, the employee must be empowered to recognize that balance is deeply personal and that employees also must be encouraged to take control of their own needs.

The Mandate for Sustainable Culture

To cement the lessons of Chapter 6, leaders must commit to four actions that shift culture from one of fear and exhaustion to one of drive and sustainability. This is the final mandate for the **Culture Gardener.** To do this they must:

1. **Inspire Employees Through Positive Leadership**. Move beyond control and manipulation. Your primary job is to ignite motivation by providing a compelling vision, psychological safety, and authentic optimism. This means regularly communicating the purpose behind the work and highlighting how each person's contribution matters.
2. **Prioritize Sustainable Value Over Long Hours.** Change the narrative around commitment. Stop equating presence with performance. Actively reward strategic results and consistent, healthy output, not self-sacrifice and burnout. Sustainable value is the only metric that truly matters.
3. **Reduce Multi-Tasking and Focus on Impactful Work**. Recognize that juggling is a detriment to organizational health. Leaders must help teams identify their most important tasks, limit the number of simultaneous projects, and encourage saying "no" to low-impact work.
4. **Foster Work-Life Balance for All.** Institutionalize the responsibility for balance. Create policies that support flexible schedules and respect personal boundaries. Crucially, leaders must model healthy work habits, taking

their own vacations and logging off on time, to empower employees to advocate for their own needs without fear.

Case Study: Harmony Foods

Harmony Foods, a regional grocery chain with deep roots in its community, had long prided itself on friendly service and reliability. However, as the company grew, so did the pressures on its workforce. Employees at all levels felt compelled to say "yes" to every request—covering extra shifts, taking on new projects, and responding to customer needs at all hours. This relentless pace, once seen as dedication, gradually led to exhaustion, high turnover, and a decline in morale.

The Cultural Challenge. When Maria Alvarez stepped in as CEO, she quickly recognized that the company's biggest obstacle wasn't competition or market trends, it was the internal culture. The always-say-yes mentality, while well-intentioned, had created a cycle of burnout. Employees felt valued only for their willingness to sacrifice personal time; managers, fearing to appear unsupportive, rarely set boundaries. The result was a workforce stretched thin, with anxiety and frustration simmering beneath the surface.

Redefining Commitment. Maria understood that true commitment should be measured by consistent value and sustainable performance, not by exhaustion. She began by openly discussing the dangers of burnout in company meetings, sharing her own experiences with overwork and the importance of rest. To shift the narrative, she introduced the weekly Happy News Meeting, a dedicated time for teams to share positive stories, celebrate small wins, and refocus on optimism. This ritual helped reframe the company's definition of success, moving away from constant busyness toward meaningful, balanced achievement.

Focus Over Fatigue. Recognizing that multitasking was diluting quality and increasing stress, Maria worked closely with managers to clarify roles and priorities. Together, they identified the most impactful tasks for each team and encouraged staff to concentrate on these, rather than juggling multiple responsibilities at once. By reducing unnecessary projects and empowering employees to say "no" to low-value work, Harmony Foods began to see improvements in both performance and job satisfaction.

Shared Responsibility and Modeling Balance. A key part of the transformation was the introduction of flexible scheduling and a renewed respect for personal boundaries. Maria didn't just set new policies—she modeled them. She made a point of leaving work on time, taking regular vacations, and discussing the importance of rest and recovery. This visible commitment from leadership gave employees permission to prioritize their own well-being without fear of judgment or reprisal.

The Results. As these changes took root, the atmosphere at Harmony Foods shifted. Anxiety and frustration gave way to renewed energy and engagement. Staff turnover dropped, customer service scores improved, and the company's reputation as a positive, supportive workplace grew. The Harmony Foods story demonstrates that when leaders prioritize balance, empower their teams, and redefine what commitment means, sustainable success naturally follows.

Summary: The Answers Are in the Culture

This chapter gives a comprehensive framework for shifting focus from seeking external solutions to cultivating the internal dynamics that truly shape an organization's success. We established that the answers to sustainable growth and high performance are not found in quick initiatives, but in the everyday behaviors, attitudes, and policies that define a company's culture.

We embraced the discipline of the *Culture Gardener*, who nurtures trust, collaboration, and accountability through small, consistent, intentional actions. We demonstrated that the healthiest cultures are those where conflict is navigated with empathy and commitment to repair, and where sustainable value is prioritized over exhaustion.

Ultimately, Chapter 6 reinforces the book's central message:

lasting transformation begins by looking inward. By fostering a positive culture rooted in trust, empowerment, balance, and authentic leadership, organizations unlock the potential that has always been in the building and waiting to be realized by those willing to lead by example.

CHAPTER 7
INCREASING EMPLOYEE ENGAGEMENT

The True Cost of Engagement: Why Teams Trump Solo Acts

The Disengagement Crisis and The Financial Imperative

Why do successful CEOs make employee engagement an absolute priority? The instinctive answer is simple: engaged employees stay. Retention should be a priority for every organization. When your best people remain, the cost of recruitment plummets, institutional knowledge deepens, and momentum is sustained. The simple goal of increasing engagement is a powerful business strategy that helps shore up the balance sheet.

The costs of high turnover and low morale are staggering. Disengaged employees don't just quietly quit by doing the minimum; they cost the organization enormous sums. Global reports estimate that disengaged employees cost the world nearly $8.8 trillion annually in lost productivity. On a micro level, the damage is equally acute:

- **Replacement Cost.** The cost of replacing a single mid-level employee ranges from 100% to 150% of their annual salary. This includes recruiting fees, onboarding, training, and the lost productivity during the vacancy. For highly specialized or executive roles, this cost can soar up to 200% or more as the lost institutional knowledge takes a long time to replace.
- **Productivity Gap.** Teams with highly engaged members are approximately 23% more productive than those with low engagement. This massive gap translates directly into lost revenue potential.
- **Absenteeism and Error.** Disengaged employees are far more likely to miss work and make mistakes, leading to quality control issues, customer complaints, and expensive rework. Unscheduled absences alone can cost thousands of dollars per employee annually.

This makes the investment in engagement not a soft HR initiative, but a mandatory financial defense.

The Hidden Iceberg: Intangible Costs of Disengagement

The costs listed above are the *visible* portion of the iceberg. The most insidious damage comes from the long-term, intangible effects that erode the company's ability to compete and innovate:

1. **Loss of Institutional Knowledge (The Brain Drain).** When senior, experienced employees—the custodians of specialized client knowledge, system histories, and process shortcuts—depart, that knowledge is not recoverable. New employees must rebuild the context from scratch, leading to slower innovation and increased risk of failure or error. This loss is often the single most expensive hidden cost.
2. **Reputational Damage and Employer Brand.** High employee turnover signals to the market that the

organization is beset with instability. It harms the employer brand, making future recruitment harder. Potential top talent, seeing high churn, will assume the company culture is toxic, forcing the organization to settle for lower-quality candidates and further perpetuating the cycle of underperformance.
3. **Diminished Discretionary Effort.** An engaged employee offers discretionary effort, the energy, creativity, and commitment they *choose* to give beyond the minimum required. Disengagement eliminates this. When employees only do the bare minimum, all opportunities for breakthrough innovation, rapid problem-solving, and superior customer service vanish. This loss of competitive edge is often fatal in fast-moving industries.

The Problem with Paying for Partial Success

Despite the clear mandate for collective success, many leaders fall into a familiar and costly trap: rewarding individual performance within organizations that rely entirely on teams.

On paper, individual bonuses appear motivational, designed to spur top performers to greater heights. However, in practice, this approach often drives internal competition, diminished collaboration, and strategic misalignment. When the majority of an organization's work is inter-dependent, requiring sales, operations, finance, and product development to function as one seamless system, incentivizing individuals creates a conflict of interest.

The Zero-Sum Game: Why Individual Incentives Undermine Collaboration

The flaw in the traditional individual bonus model is that it forces employees into a zero-sum game mentality. If one person's success is seen as potentially reducing the resources or recognition available to another, the natural response is to compete, not collaborate. This toxic dynamic manifests in specific, measurable organizational friction:

- **Resource Hoarding.** Employees are incentivized to conceal critical information, hide process shortcuts, or guard client relationships, viewing these assets as *personal keys* to their bonus, rather than *organizational assets* for collective growth. This stifles knowledge transfer and slows down the entire system.
- **The Silo Mentality.** Individual incentives often lead to the creation of departmental or personal silos. A team may achieve its target, but in doing so they may inadvertently create massive downstream problems for another department, for example, Sales landing a complicated deal that Operations cannot handle, yet Sales gets the bonus. This is the definition of partial success—achieving one metric at the expense of overall business health.
- **Ethical Erosion.** When the financial stakes are high, individual metrics can tempt employees to prioritize their paycheck over the company's long-term reputation or ethical guidelines, leading to corner-cutting and compliance risks.

The traditional model essentially incentivizes employees to pursue metrics that benefit their paycheck, even if those actions detract from the overall health of the business. You are left paying for performance that is only partially successful and, in the worst cases, actively destructive to collective momentum.

The Solution: The WiiN Mandate and Shared Destiny

The solution is clear: stop rewarding individuals in a vacuum and start incentivizing the group.

When incentive structures are based on collective wins, they create a powerful culture of collaboration and shared destiny. A team working together for a shared reward will always move your business further than any individual ever could. This is the WiiN (What's in it for the Network) Mandate. In WiiN, you align the reward mechanism with the overarching strategic goal.

The Benefits of Collective Incentives

1. **Increased Trust and Openness.** When everyone's bonus depends on the team's shared outcome, people are naturally motivated to help each other succeed. Knowledge is shared freely, and colleagues proactively assist in solving problems, recognizing that lifting others directly benefits themselves.
2. **Effective Problem-Solving**. Collective incentives force teams to look beyond their own boundaries. For example, rather than simply measuring how many leads the marketing team generates (an individual metric), the team is measured on the combined metric of Marketing-Qualified Leads that convert to Revenue (a collective metric spanning Marketing and Sales). This shared accountability fosters genuine partnership in solving systemic issues.
3. **Reinforcement of Psychological Safety**. The collective reward structure acts as a financial layer of psychological safety. When mistakes happen, the focus shifts from finding fault to finding a fix because a collective failure impacts everyone. This reinforces the culture of learning and reduces the fear of personal risk-taking.

Moving to a Hybrid Model: Combining the Best of Both Worlds

While collective incentives are paramount in team-based environments, it would be a mistake to eliminate individual recognition entirely. Highly effective organizations employ a hybrid model that maximizes the strengths of both, typically structured as follows:

1. **Foundation (70-80%).** The majority of incentive compensation is tied to collective, measurable outcomes (e.g., company profit, department goal achievement, team-level KPIs). This is the structural cement that ensures all eyes are fixed on the overarching organizational priorities.
2. **Individual Component (20-30%).** A smaller portion is reserved for individual recognition. This should not be based solely on metrics but on contributions that support the collective culture, such as mentorship, leadership development, proactive problem identification, or demonstrating the core company values. This system allows leaders to recognize exceptional effort and value-driven behavior without accidentally encouraging resource hoarding or internal sabotage.

By structuring incentives this way, you send a clear message that your personal success is inseparable from the collective success. This single change—moving from rewarding partial success to celebrating shared destiny—is one of the most powerful levers a leader can pull to drive genuine engagement and build long-term organizational health.

Beyond the Paycheck: The Power of Contribution

While group incentives are the necessary structural component, they are not the blueprint. The true, most frequently overlooked reason for losing great people is they feel a profound lack of meaningful contribution.

The best employees crave more than a steady job; they want to be integral to the solution. They need autonomy and influence. When leaders fail to seek input, delegate critical tasks, or invite top talent into strategic discussions, they communicate a powerful, toxic signal that translates as: "Your best thinking is not valued here." This psychological withdrawal is the precursor to resignation.

To achieve true engagement, the lesson is twofold. Don't just pay them well, empower them to contribute meaningfully and reward them for collective success.

Leading Change with Purpose: The Power of Internal Narrative

The structural shift to team-based rewards must be paired with an equally powerful shift in how leaders communicate change. Getting employees truly on board begins with understanding what genuinely excites people, and it is not the data. It is the story.

Data Drives Decisions, Stories Drive People

We must accept that data drives decisions, but stories drive people. While analytics are essential for strategic direction, they do not ignite passion. The role of the leader is to translate the cold logic of the balance sheet into the compelling drama of the mission. When the mission is clear, teams don't just execute instructions, they innovate and excel.

Ignoring this human element leads to two severe consequences:

1. **The Passion Deficit.** When data is presented without the narrative of why this matters, employees respond with compliance, not commitment. They do the minimum necessary to avoid scrutiny.
2. **The Cycle of Cynicism.** Making a change just for the sake of change breeds burnout and fatigue, teaching employees to simply wait it out. This institutional memory of non-purposeful change is toxic.

The only way to overcome this fatigue is to commit to a **Purpose-**

Driven Change Mandate. This means committing to change that makes a difference. This is what truly ignites purpose.

Four Disciplines for Purposeful Change

Translating this philosophy into a high-engagement environment requires deliberate and continuous action from the leader.

1. Launch with Narrative: Communicate Change with Purpose and Story

Most organizational changes fail because of the failure to communicate. Leaders must communicate change with purpose and story. The act of explaining the reasons behind a task or change invests employees *in* that task. When they understand *why* their action is critical, they bring creativity and renewed effort, transforming an instruction into an investment.

2. Activate the Inner Circle: Engage Key Employees Early for Buy-In

To reduce friction and maximize adoption, you must engage key employees early for buy-in. Bring influential individuals into the planning phase before the final decision is public. By asking for their input on *how* to implement the change (the practical application of Appreciative Inquiry), you gain superior, practical execution plans and convert potential skeptics into powerful internal ambassadors for the change.

3. Campaign for Change: Practice Internal Marketing

Employee engagement is a continuous relationship. Leaders must practice internal marketing to continuously sell the vision and value proposition. Treat every major change as a campaign. Build excitement, share the vision, and continuously highlight the benefits using multiple channels. Celebrate early wins to ensure employees remain connected to the collective momentum.

4. Foster Collective Ownership: Create Opportunities for Contribution

The most effective action step for retention is ensuring your top talent feels indispensable. You must create opportunities for employee contribution by delegating complex, high-leverage problems. When employees feel their expertise is not just welcomed but necessary for the company's future, they invest emotionally in a way no compensation plan can replicate.

The Foundation of Trust and Accountability

Trust: The Single Biggest Accelerator

Trust is the single biggest accelerator for any team. Without it, hesitation, low morale, and underperformance take root. When trust is present, people become more committed, more creative, and far more willing to take ownership. The path to building enduring trust requires daily, intentional practice. To that this:

- **Say What You Mean, Mean What You Say.** Consistency and integrity in your words and actions are the bedrock of security.
- **Be a Consistent Leader.** Fairness is essential. Consistency is the currency of respect. Leaders who change the rules based on the employee or the mood of the day destroy trust instantly.
- **Give Them the Reins.** Empower your team to make decisions within their defined scope, thus actively signaling your absolute trust in their potential.

The Low Engagement Trap and Psychological Safety

The symptoms of low engagement—the **Low Engagement Trap**—begin with the collapse of trust. Without trust, you get hesitation, low morale, and underperformance. This leads to the **Breakdown of Accountability,** where the least effective employees can silently take control of operations, setting the lowest acceptable standard.

The solution is for the leader to be the change agent and the solutions provider by establishing **Psychological Safety**—the shared belief that the team is safe for personal risk-taking.

Fostering Psychological Safety: The Engine of Discretionary Effort

Psychological safety is not about being nice. It is about establishing a culture where employees feel comfortable with personal risk-taking, specifically, the risks of speaking up, asking questions, admitting mistakes, and respectfully challenging the status quo. This is the condition that unlocks discretionary effort.

Managerial Model for Psychological Safety

- **Frame the Work as a Learning Problem.** When discussing a challenge, frame it as a collective learning opportunity rather than a failure in execution. For example, instead of "Who messed up the launch?" ask, "What did we collectively learn from this launch process that we can improve?"
- **Embrace Productive Conflict.** Explicitly state that disagreement is welcomed only if it is focused on the process or idea, not the person. Leaders must model this by welcoming challenges and thanking the employee for raising the issue, even when the final decision remains unchanged.

- **Respond Constructively to Failure.** When a mistake occurs, focus on the "why" in the system, not the "who" in the chair. To normalize imperfection, leaders must share their own failures as learning moments. This is the direct countermeasure to the culture of *impression management* where employees hide errors to protect their personal reputation.

The Power of Appreciative Inquiry: Shifting from Deficit to Design

The most effective method for instilling this psychological safety and for capturing the boundless energy of discretionary effort is through Appreciative Inquiry (AI). This methodology is a radical departure from traditional, deficit-based management, which often paralyzes teams in a cycle of blame and fatigue.

Escaping the Deficit Trap

Most efforts at improving an organization start with the question: "What is broken? What are the gaps, the failures, and the problems?" This deficit-based approach is inherently demotivating. It trains employees to focus on weakness, past failures, and deficiencies. This drains emotional energy and reinforces the fear of failure. It creates a culture of fixing rather than a culture of creating.

Appreciative Inquiry flips this perspective entirely. Instead of focusing on "what is broken?" (the deficit), AI shifts the conversation to "what already works well?" By focusing on the organization's existing strengths, peak performance moments, and successes, AI generates a positive emotional charge, and this is a powerful resource proven to unlock creativity, optimism, and kickstart a collective willingness to innovate.

The 4-D Cycle: A Roadmap to Shared Destiny

AI follows a clear, powerful **4-D Cycle** to move from past success to future design, making every employee an active participant in the organizational narrative through:

1. **Discovery (The Best of What Is).** This phase is dedicated to interviewing employees, customers, and partners to uncover and celebrate peak times of organizational success and excellence. The main question guiding this phase is: "What was the organization at its best?" The leader facilitates deep storytelling, gathering powerful narratives about successful collaborations, innovative breakthroughs, and moments where the team truly felt connected and proud.
    - **Action Example.** Conduct interviews using prompts like: "Describe a project where you felt the most energized and successful. What factors—people, processes, or resources—made that success possible?"
2. **Dream (Imagining What Could Be).** Using the positive energy and discovered strengths from the first phase, this phase encourages employees to envision the ideal future based on those peak experiences. This is the opportunity to think expansively, unconstrained by current limitations. The central question is. "If you had three wishes, what would the company look like, leveraging the strengths we identified in Discovery?" This aligns individual aspiration with organizational potential.
    - **Action Example.** Holding visioning sessions where teams create mood boards or headlines describing the company five years from now, exclusively utilizing its greatest historical strengths.
3. **Design (Determining What Should Be).** In this critical stage, the team co-constructs provocative propositions— bold, affirmative statements of what the organization *will be*

when it operates from its highest potential. These are not mission statements; they are practical, present-tense declarations that challenge the status quo and act as blueprints for the future. The design must be measurable and inspiring.
   - **Action Example**. Transitioning successful narratives into actionable principles, such as: "We are a company where every promotion is a successful transition because we proactively provide coaching and mentorship **before** the job change," or "Our culture is one of fearless learning, where failure is celebrated as data for innovation."
4. **Destiny / Deliver (Sustaining What Will Be).** In the final phase, employees take inspired action to live in the Design. The provocative propositions become the filter for every new strategy, process, and interaction. Because the team designed the future themselves based on their own best experiences, there is built-in commitment and intrinsic motivation to execute.
   - **Action Example.** Implementing new communication protocols designed in the Design phase and setting up peer-to-peer accountability groups to ensure the provocative propositions become daily operational reality.

AI and the Architect of Safe Accountability

By using AI, the leader is no longer just the problem-identifier or the chief fixer of deficiencies. They are now the architect of a positive, empowering space.

Appreciative Inquiry establishes a safe accountability environment where clear, unambiguous standards protect the emotional investment employees have made in the outcome. Employees are accountable to the collective vision they helped create, reducing the natural resistance to top-down directives. When accountability is tied to shared success, it reinforces psychological safety because the goal is no longer about avoiding punishment but about achieving the desired, co-created future. This framework ensures that creativity, risk-taking and innovation thrive, directly translating into high-level discretionary effort.

The Leader's Mandate: The Accountability Accelerator

To transform culture, the leader must master four specific mechanics.

Action Step	How to Execute (The Mechanics)	The Strategic Why
1. Lead by Example	**Model the Culture:** Demonstrate the behaviors, attitudes, and accountability you expect. Take initiative in solving problems, not just identifying them.	**The Source of Momentum:** Engagement starts with leadership. When you model commitment, it sets the standard and inspires others to follow, reducing managerial friction.
2. Build & Maintain Trust	**Practice Radical Transparency:** Communicate openly and be consistent and fair. Follow through on promises and admit mistakes when they happen.	**The Accelerator of Trust:** Trust is the single biggest accelerator for any team. Without it, hesitation and political maneuvering take root.
3. Invite & Empower	**Integrate Contribution:** Use Appreciative Inquiry to solicit and integrate ideas. Encourage participation in problem-solving and decision-making.	**The Power of Emotional Investment:** When employees feel safe to contribute, they become emotionally invested in outcomes. Engaging them to solve problems transforms culture.
4. Instill Clear Accountability	**Enforce Clear Standards:** Define roles and expectations clearly. Set measurable goals and address underperformance promptly and constructively.	**The Clarity of Accountability:** Accountability drives performance. Clear standards transform operations from chaotic to highly effective and ensure that high performers are not carrying underperformers.

Recognition and Growth: The Compounding Value of Investment

The final theme is **Recognition**, which must be viewed as an ongoing investment in future capability, not just a reward for past success.

The Power of Proactive Recognition

Employees feel most valued when they feel seen. When they are visible. To that end, show your employees you value them in tangible, consistent ways. True recognition is to recognize what an employee can contribute both before and after the fact.

- **Proactive Recognition.** Before the work even begins, recognize your employees by seeking their input and ask: "What do you think?" This empowers them and builds emotional investment.
- **Managing Cultural Drag.** Stop trying to solve the problem of the few and start celebrating the efforts of the many. By consistently shining a light on hard work and dedication, you elevate the positive cultural dynamic, making it difficult for negativity and low effort to thrive. Recognition naturally encourages more success and downplays negative contributions.

Investing in Growth and Capability: The ROI Case

The real way to keep your best employees is not just by saying thank you, but by strategically investing in them through better pay, benefits, or professional development. A valued employee is one whose career trajectory is prioritized by the organization.

- **Mentorship ROI.** Mentorship is not a perk; it is a proven talent accelerator. Employees involved in mentoring

programs have up to 50% higher retention rates than those not involved. Furthermore, companies with structured mentoring programs often report significantly higher profits than those without. Mentees are five times more likely to advance their careers, and mentors are six times more likely to be promoted.
- **Soft Skills as a Tool**. Leaders must reject the notion of thinking soft skills are innate. Soft skills—such as emotional intelligence, communication, and seamless teamwork—are learnable, powerful tools that dramatically improve collective outcomes. Studies show that most employees who receive soft skills training report that it positively impacted their performance. Investing in these skills is a direct investment in the reduction of internal friction.
- **Strategic Training**. To prevent training from being a one-off event, sustainable behavior change requires a continuous, intentional approach. To do this you must:
  1. **Align**. Link every training initiative to specific, measurable, strategic business goals. If it does not support a key objective, eliminate it.
  2. **Act**. Deliver training effectively and embed it in daily work through follow-up coaching, peer reinforcement, and managerial accountability.
  3. **Audit**. Continuously measure the impact of the program (e.g., skill adoption, reduction in customer complaints) long after it's completed to prove ROI and to drive continuous improvement.

Promoting for Success: The Dual Career Track Model

The classic management failure is the **Peter Principle,** where star technical performers are promoted into management roles without proper training, leading to them struggling at their level of incompetence. This destroys the individual's confidence and the team's faith in leadership.

The solution is the **Dual Career Track Model**.

Track	Focus	Reward Mechanism	Goal
Management Track	Leadership, coaching, strategy, budget, delegation.	Promotions based on team performance and strategic impact.	Developing generalists who excel at managing people and resources.
Technical Track	Deep, specialized expertise, complex problem-solving, innovation, system architecture.	Promotions (e.g., Senior Principal, Fellow) based on depth of knowledge and technical innovation, with equivalent salary and title prestige to management roles.	Developing specialists who excel at managing complexity and knowledge.

Implementation Steps

1. **Assess Potential**. Focus the management promotion process on aptitude for leadership and coaching (soft skills), not solely on past technical performance.
2. **Pre-emptive Training.** Invest in leadership training before promotion. Provide management courses, mentorship, and temporary acting roles before the title change is made permanent.
3. **Formalize the Dual Path.** Create clear, documented promotion criteria for both tracks, ensuring the top rung of the Technical Track is compensated and valued equally to the top rung of the Management Track. This eliminates the financial incentive to take a management role for the wrong reasons.

Case Studies: Principles in Practice

Case Study A: Summit Financial Group (Trust and Contribution)

The journey of Summit Financial Group (SFG), a mid-sized asset management firm, provides a clear, practical demonstration of the power of trust and Appreciative Inquiry (AI) to reverse cultural stagnation.

The Problem: The Erosion of Discretionary Effort

For years, SFG had operated on a performance review system that heavily penalized mistakes. The CEO, Alex Morgan, observed a creeping cautious compliance throughout the firm. Employees were technically proficient, but they consistently did the absolute minimum. Critical reporting was slow, innovation was non-existent, and high-potential talent was leaving, citing a "lack of voice" and a "fear of failure." The culture was characterized by silent silos, high managerial oversight, and a systemic lack of trust.

The Solution: Launching the Discovery Phase

Facing stagnant engagement scores, CEO Alex Morgan committed to a radical shift. He initiated an AI process, committing publicly to radical transparency and consistency—the foundations of trust. He communicated that the goal was not to assign blame for past mistakes, but to learn from past successes.

He launched the Discovery phase of Appreciative Inquiry with a firm-wide invitation, asking employees to share stories of Summit Financial at its very best. Morgan deliberately hosted small-group listening sessions where he, the CEO, spent hours documenting moments when teams felt *most* proud, *most* effective, and *most* energized. The key finding was that SFG excelled when junior staff were given direct input on client problems, proving that expertise was distributed, not centralized.

Empowering Contribution: The Story of Taylor Kim

This new atmosphere of inquiry immediately paid dividends. In the high-pressure environment of the back office, the slow, manual process for quarterly portfolio reconciliation was a constant source of error and overtime.

A junior analyst named Taylor Kim, who had always kept her head down for fear of making waves, finally felt safe enough to speak up. She did not complain about the process; instead, she leveraged the AI framework to submit a Dream proposal based on a successful, one-off project she had executed personally. Her idea suggested an innovative new workflow—a series of scripts and automation hooks that could cut the reconciliation time by 40% while dramatically reducing human error.

Morgan's executive team did not debate or delay. They publicly recognized Taylor's proactive contribution and immediately empowered a small cross-functional team, led by Taylor, to implement the changes. By giving Taylor the reins and publicly backing her proposal, they earned their emotional investment. Her success became a visible, celebrated proof point that "Your best thinking is valued here."

The Shift to Ownership: Instilling Safe Accountability

As trust grew, the organization moved to solidify the Design and Destiny phases of AI, leading to the institutionalization of Safe Accountability.

1. **Roles were Clarified**. The provocative propositions (the Design) defined clear, unambiguous standards for

communication and teamwork, creating a framework where people knew exactly what was expected.
2. **Mistakes were Reframed**. The leadership team adopted a policy where process mistakes were treated as learning opportunities rather than reasons for blame, reinforcing psychological safety. When a new system deployment went wrong, Morgan focused the post-mortem entirely on systemic flaws, asking: "What was missing from our review process?" instead of "Who signed off on this error?"
3. **The Result.** Summit Financial Group's culture shifted from cautious compliance (doing the minimum to avoid punishment) to enthusiastic ownership (taking strategic risks and investing energy to achieve the collective vision). This cultural transformation was measurable. Staff turnover for high-potential employees dropped by 15% within the first year, proving that the answer to engagement lies in developing trust and fostering meaningful contribution.

Case Study B: Horizon Health Systems (Proactive Investment)

At Horizon Health Systems (HHS), a large regional hospital network, the executive team recognized they were facing a significant value deficit. High performers felt taken for granted, and the promotion structure was creating constant internal friction. Recognition was sporadic, and promoted individuals into management were failing, validating the classic organizational dread of the Peter Principle.

CEO Susan Chen launched a comprehensive initiative focused on appreciation, professional development, and strategic career planning. In doing this, she changed the way the company saw recognition, treating it as an active investment in what employees could achieve in the future.

The Double-Duty Recognition Strategy

Chen began with a two-pronged strategy to elevate visibility and validate expertise, using:

1. **Public, Visible Recognition (After the Fact).** The standard practice of celebrating milestones was enhanced with highly visible, public platforms focused on specific, value-driven contributions (e.g., recognizing a team for improving patient flow time by X%, not just for having a great month).
2. **Proactive Recognition (Before the Fact).** Critically, managers were trained to practice proactive recognition by inviting team members into the planning stages of new project *before* the project was launched. This demonstrated trust in their intellect.

This shift was powerful. When junior administrator Jamal Rivers identified a systemic scheduling inefficiency, he was not just rewarded for his observation; he was immediately brought into the executive planning session to help design the fix. By trusting him with a high-leverage problem, they proved their respect for his expertise. Jamal's proposal for a new scheduling system was considered and implemented, and he became the subject matter expert driving the rollout.

Strategic Development: The Power of Mentorship and Soft Skills

HHS formalized its commitment to development, rejecting the idea that training was merely a cost center. They viewed it as the ultimate retention tool.

- **Mentorship became a Cornerstone.** A structured, formal mentorship program was launched, pairing high-potential employees (like Jamal) with seasoned leaders. This not only

accelerated the mentee's growth but also provided the mentor with new insights and perspectives, aligning with the evidence that both parties experienced a significant boost in retention and career trajectory.
- **The Investment in Soft Skills.** Recognizing that the friction points in the system were often behavioral, not technical, Chen invested heavily in soft skills training. She championed the idea that skills like emotional intelligence, complex communication, and conflict resolution are learnable, powerful tools for reducing internal friction and improving collective outcomes. The training was not a one-off event but was embedded, reinforced, and measured to ensure sustained behavioral change and maximum ROI.

Avoiding the Peter Principle: Implementing the Dual Career Track

The most significant strategic innovation at HHS was the implementation of the **Dual Career Track Model** to specifically address the costly failure of the **Peter Principle** (referring to the promotion of a high performer into a management role for which they are ill-suited).

The HR structure was fundamentally altered by creating:

- **Two Equal Ladders.** HHS created parallel tracks. These were the Management/Leadership Track and the Technical/Expert Track.
- **Equal Value, Different Focus.** The company adjusted the pay scales, job titles (like "Principal Fellow" instead of "Manager"), and organizational status for the top technical positions to be equal to those in the Management Track. This ensured that talented employees—such as brilliant engineers or clinicians—no longer had to take a management job just to earn a higher income.
- **Pre-emptive Training**. Promotions were managed with a new strategic mindset. Leadership aptitude was prioritized

for the Management Track, and intensive leadership training (including coaching, budgeting, and performance management) was provided before the promotion was made permanent. Managers assessed potential and readiness, not just past performance metrics.

When Jamal Rivers was ready to advance, he was offered a choice to pursue the **Management Track** with required pre-promotion training or advance along the **Technical Track** to become a **Principal Process Architect.** He chose the technical path, leveraging his deep system knowledge to optimize the entire network's efficiency, a job that was now correctly compensated and valued, contributing far more to the bottom line than a general managerial role would have.

The ultimate result at Horizon Health Systems was a dramatic shift in cultural health and organizational capability. The deliberate, visible investment in its people fueled organic growth and retention, proving that when leaders celebrate contributions and proactively prepare employees for the future, the organization flourishes.

Summary: The Full Engagement Framework

The final message of this chapter is clear: the answers to scaling upward are found by looking inward. By implementing the framework of **Group Incentives, Purposeful Communication, Trust, Accountability,** and **Proactive Recognition**, leaders unlock the full potential of their teams and build organizations where people thrive.

Final Action Checklist: The Engagement Blueprint

Focus Area	Critical Action Steps
Structural Alignment	Shift incentives to **collective wins (WiiN)**. Eliminate rewards for partial individual success that breed internal competition.
Cultural Mandate	**Lead with Story:** Communicate the *why* and the *purpose* behind all change to inspire commitment and discretionary effort.
Trust & Accountability	**Establish Psychological Safety**. Use **Appreciative Inquiry** to build solutions from existing strengths, instilling **safe, clear accountability**.
Contribution & Value	**Recognize Contributions Before & After the Fact:** Proactively invite employee expertise into problem-solving and publicly celebrate success.
Talent Development	**Invest in Mentorship** and **Soft Skills** as strategic tools. Make training **Continuous and Strategic** (Align, Act, Audit).
Career Strategy	Implement a **Dual Career Track Model**. **Pre-emptively train** for new roles, focusing on potential to avoid the Peter Principle.

CHAPTER 8
YOUR SECRET GROWTH DRIVER: SECOND CHANCE EMPLOYMENT

In this chapter, we reveal a powerful, often overlooked strategy for scaling and growing your business: second-chance employment. This initiative is far more than a social program; it is a profound business model innovation that directly addresses one of the modern CEO's most critical obstacles—talent scarcity.

This strategy is about expanding your addressable talent market to include individuals whose past justice-involvement often makes them highly motivated, loyal, and reliable employees.

By intentionally tapping into this under-served and under-used talent pool (justice-impacted individuals seeking a fresh start) businesses can unlock a high level of loyalty, productivity, and reliability within their workforce. These candidates possess a unique perspective forged by adversity, often bringing an exceptional work ethic and deep appreciation for opportunity that translates directly into lower turnover and higher engagement.

Implementing a second-chance employment program isn't a task to be taken lightly; it requires a systemic change in culture and process. It does come with specific, navigable challenges. These employees thrive with enhanced support, a balanced and non-toxic work environment, and meaningful incentives to stay engaged, but the returns on this investment are exponential.

Fortunately, the leadership techniques, positive culture-building strategies, and employee engagement methods we've outlined throughout this book are precisely the tools required to meet these needs seamlessly.

Effective leadership and an engaged, positive workplace culture are essential for harnessing the full potential of second-chance employees, providing the business with a workforce that is often more eager, more loyal, and significantly more productive than traditional hires.

By integrating this model into your core strategy, you gain a decisive competitive edge, turning this talent pool into your secret weapon for sustainable growth.

Walk the Talk—Confronting the Leadership Barrier

The success of a second-chance employment program starts and ends with the genuine commitment of its leadership. It is not enough to simply *claim* to support second chance hiring; true leadership demands active and continuous dismantling of the barriers created by acknowledged or unconscious biases that often reside silently within the leadership suite itself. These subtle biases can undermine the program before it even starts, creating internal resistance that defeats the very purpose you claim to champion.

Unmasking Leadership Bias: The Subtlety of Sabotage

A leader's role is not simply to sign off on the initiative; it is to actively dismantle the internal and external barriers that prevent deserving candidates from succeeding. When leaders are unaware of

YOUR SECRET GROWTH DRIVER: SECOND CHANCE EMPLOYME...

their own cognitive shortcuts, they allow cultural inertia to sabotage the program's integrity.

Consider the pervasive damage caused by **confirmation bias.** A manager seeking proof that the program will fail will inevitably find it. They'll seize on one minor incident—an employee being late, a small procedural mistake—to confirm their existing negative stereotypes and ignore all metrics that demonstrate high performance or strong retention.

This intellectual selectivity often leads to the program's premature abandonment, creating a self-fulfilling prophecy of failure long before the long-term Return on Investment (ROI) is realized. This is a failure of leadership, not talent.

Equally damaging is **affinity bias,** which causes leaders to equate professionalism or trust only with candidates who share a conventional, non-justice-involved background. This translates into the so-called fit trap, where second-chance candidates are excluded during the interview or promotion phase simply because they don't fit the look.

The leader mistakenly equates unfamiliarity with risk, thereby maintaining a homogeneous and ultimately limiting corporate culture. The hiring process, intended to identify skills, becomes a process of cultural filtering.

The subtle trap of **attribution bias** creates an impossible standard for these employees. When a traditional hire makes a mistake, the event is generously attributed to a bad day, a flawed process, or external circumstances. However, when a second-chance hire commits the same mistake, the failure is often attributed solely to their criminal background or presumed character flaw.

Conversely, when they succeed, the achievement is minimized, attributed to luck or the exceptional quality of the manager. This bias effectively denies second-chance hires the same grace, mentorship, and constructive feedback routinely given to other employees, hamstringing their ability to grow and achieve their full potential.

Finally, the **savior** or **paternalistic bias** views these employees as charity cases rather than valuable, capable talent. This dangerous perspective manifests as lowered expectations, assigning menial, dead-end tasks, or over-praising basic competence that should simply be expected. This patronizing behavior limits career growth and stifles the ambition and loyalty of the very talent pool you sought to harness, turning a crucial talent pipeline into a marginalized, segregated program destined for high turnover.

Creating Awareness and Systemic Mitigation

Leadership commitment means creating a transparent environment where biases are not just discussed but systematically mitigated through policy and process. This is how you institutionalize the support the leader claims to champion.

Executive Self-Reflection and Acknowledgment

This is the first, most critical step. The CEO and all senior leaders must engage in genuine self-reflection and then publicly and explicitly acknowledge that bias exists within the organization, even at the executive level. This act of vulnerability establishes a cultural precedent for accountability and trust, signaling to the entire workforce that this initiative is being taken seriously. Without this public accountability, the initiative risks being perceived as an empty **Human Resources Mandate** that management can safely ignore.

Institutionalize Accountability

Next, you must **institutionalize accountability** by tying the program's success directly to senior management performance. KPI Alignment is crucial. That is, the retention rates, internal promotion rates, and performance ratings of second-chance employees must become key performance indicators (KPIs) for the managers who oversee them. What gets measured gets managed, and what gets managed gets executive attention.

Furthermore, assign a senior, non-HR executive to mentor and sponsor the program. This provides visible, executive-level advocacy that signals its criticality to the business model, not just its social merits.

Structured Decision-Making

To counter subjective judgment, implement **structured decision-making**. This means utilizing skills-based, standardized interviews and rigorous assessments focused entirely on core job competencies. Where legally and practically feasible, use blind resume reviews to redact identifying details related to background until the final offer stage. This removes the opportunity for unconscious bias to enter the process early, ensuring decisions are data driven.

Managerial Training

Finally, dedicate resources to **managerial training**, shifting from fixer to coach. Leaders must be trained to treat second-chance employees not as problems to be solved, but as high-potential individuals to be coached. This means delivering equal feedback at the same level of rigorous, constructive mentorship provided to traditional hires; lowered expectations are a form of soft bigotry that prevents growth.

Training must also equip managers to maintain appropriate boundaries and confidentiality, focusing entirely on the employee's current performance and future potential, not their past. When a leader actively works to challenge these implicit biases, they demonstrate that their commitment is a fundamental operating principle, transforming a second-chance program into a first-rate, scalable talent strategy.

The Economics of Opportunity —Calculating the ROI

While the ethical case for second-chance employment is compelling, the commitment must be sustained by clear financial results. The returns on this investment are often exponential, driven by factors that traditional recruiting metrics fail to capture. The true ROI lies in the substantial cost reductions associated with talent retention and performance.

The Hidden Cost of Churn

Most businesses accept high employee turnover as an unavoidable cost of doing business, especially in high-growth or entry-level departments. However, the cost of churn—including recruitment fees, onboarding time, lost productivity during training, and decreased morale—can easily exceed 150% of an employee's salary.

Second-chance employees directly attack this financial drain. Driven by a deep appreciation for the opportunity, this talent pool consistently demonstrates retention rates up to 40% higher than those of traditional hires in comparable roles.

This translates into hundreds of thousands of dollars saved annually. By viewing second-chance employment as an aggressive retention strategy, you are not just investing in people; you are buying financial stability and dramatically lowering your operational overhead.

The Loyalty Dividend and Discretionary Effort

Beyond simple retention, the loyalty demonstrated by justice-impacted employees delivers a loyalty dividend—a concept rooted in discretionary effort.

Discretionary effort is the willingness of an employee to give more than the minimum required by their job description. Because second-chance employees often view their role as a pillar of stability for their lives, they exhibit higher levels of motivation, leading to:

- **Reduced Absenteeism.** They prioritize showing up and being reliable.
- **Proactive Problem-Solving.** They are more likely to flag process flaws or take initiative to find a solution, as they see the company's success directly tied to their own.
- **High Engagement.** This intrinsic motivation fuels productivity gains that outstrip those of less engaged traditional employees.

The combination of higher retention and higher discretionary effort means your investment in training and development yields a far greater, more enduring return, making this talent segment financially superior in the long run.

Strategic Integration— Talent Pipeline by Design

For second-chance employment to be a true growth driver, it cannot operate as a segregated HR function; it must be a fully integrated component of your talent acquisition strategy and your capacity planning.

Mapping the Program to Capacity Needs

Successful companies map their second-chance program directly to their most pressing business needs, often those high-turnover, essential roles where stability is paramount to scaling.

1. **Identify High-Friction Roles.** Pinpoint departments (like warehouse operations, entry-level manufacturing, or

customer support centers) that suffer from chronic turnover. These are the immediate targets, as the high loyalty of second-chance hires will deliver instant stability and a measurable reduction in recruitment costs.
2. **Establish Growth Pathways.** Avoid the paternalistic mistake of assigning dead-end jobs. The system must include clear, measurable paths for internal promotion and upskilling. By offering training in high-value skills (e.g., machinery certification, software proficiency, supervisory roles), you convert a motivated new hire into a long-term, specialized asset. The retention rate for second-chance employees increases dramatically when they see a clear career trajectory.

Leveraging External Ecosystems

A CEO cannot manage the entire reintegration process alone. The key to successful, scalable implementation is to leverage the robust external ecosystem designed to support this population. To do so create:

- **Formal Pipeline Partnerships.** Establish official, vetted relationships with non-profits, halfway houses, and state workforce agencies that specialize in re-entry. These partners provide pre-vetted candidates who are often job-ready and, crucially, offer the wraparound support (housing, therapy, financial coaching) that the company is neither equipped nor obligated to provide.
- **Federal Tax Incentives.** Use government programs designed to encourage this hiring. The **Work Opportunity Tax Credit (WOTC)** and similar state programs offer significant tax benefits for hiring individuals from targeted groups, including those who were formerly incarcerated. These financial incentives can substantially offset the initial costs of training and

onboarding, transforming the program into an immediate, tax-advantaged win.

The Cultural Force Multiplier

When implemented with genuine commitment from the CEO, second-chance employment acts as a powerful cultural force multiplier, benefiting every employee, not just the new hires.

Redefining Corporate Values in Action

Culture is built not on what the CEO *says* they believe, but on what the company rewards and tolerates. A successful second-chance program is the ultimate display of corporate values in action. When existing employees see the company investing time and resources into mentoring individuals with a past, they internalize a deeper sense of mission and purpose.

This visible commitment translates directly into a more empathetic and supportive workplace for all. Existing employees begin to act as mentors and coaches, finding a renewed sense of purpose that combats cynicism and boosts overall morale.

This organic shift transforms your culture from one of subtle resistance to one of shared support and accountability, strengthening the organizational bonds that underpin resilience and scaling.

The Power of Empathy and Perspective

Second-chance employees, when properly integrated, bring a valuable diversity of thought and life experience. Their unique perspective forged by adversity can be a powerful antidote to organizational complacency. They often challenge assumptions about efficiency, risk, and resource utilization, seeing opportunities for process improvement that established employees overlook.

This forced introspection and rise in empathy creates a more robust internal environment. When a team operates with high empathy and views mistakes as data points for systemic improvement (rather than personal failings), it dramatically improves cross-functional collaboration and speeds up the entire problem-solving cycle, the very deft hand required to scale successfully.

Debunking the Myths— Addressing Common Concerns

While the strategic case is clear, successful implementation requires proactively addressing the very real operational and human concerns that can stall or derail the program. These obstacles, rooted in fear and unfamiliarity, are all solvable with transparent policies and data-driven counterarguments.

Safety Concerns and Perceived Risk

The most immediate and understandable objection relates to the well-being of the current team and the company's financial liability.

Worries about workplace safety are natural, but they are often based on outdated assumptions and media sensationalism. Leaders must stress that background checks are standard procedure, and that candidates for roles with specific safety, security, or financial exposure requirements are meticulously vetted.

The reality is that most justice-impacted individuals are not violent offenders, and their recidivism rates drop dramatically with stable employment. Furthermore, the commitment and loyalty demonstrated by these hires often translates into a more stable, low-turnover environment, which inherently improves safety and morale compared to the chaos of constant churn in high-turnover departments.

The fear of increased liability or risk is a common boardroom protest, but the counterargument is financial and legal. Many states and localities offer Federal Bonding Programs (FBP) that protect employers against losses due to employee theft, fraud, or dishonesty, often at no cost.

This government-backed protection effectively mitigates the financial risk. Strategically, the greater risk to the business is the cost of constant talent scarcity and the erosion of brand reputation due to a lack of social responsibility. By responsibly integrating this talent pool, the company is managing its most pressing existential risk: a competitive labor market.

Managing Cultural Resistance and Integration

Successfully integrating second-chance hires requires navigating resistance and discomfort from existing staff.

It's critical to acknowledge that other employees may feel uneasy or resistant to change. This discomfort is best managed not through mandates, but through communication and education. Leaders should host focused, optional town halls explaining the *why* of the program—framing it not as a risk, but as an expression of the company's core values and a solution to talent shortages.

When employees understand the commitment and mentorship framework, their resistance often turns to support. The focus must remain laser-sharp on the individual's current performance and future contribution, not their past.

To combat bias and stereotypes—which challenge these programs with persistent negative assumptions—introduce direct, personal exposure wherever possible. Sharing anonymous success stories, inviting second-chance employees to speak (voluntarily) about their journey, and celebrating their contributions publicly can quickly dissolve generalized stereotypes. Leaders must use their platform to model the correct behavior, consistently showcasing that character, work ethic, and determination are the only metrics that matter.

The final hurdle is the practical difficulty in creating a truly inclusive environment. This isn't solved by a single orientation; it requires a systemic approach. It demands the creation of formal mentorship programs where current employees are incentivized and trained to act as peer sponsors and ensuring that disciplinary and promotion processes are transparent and applied equally to all staff. When inclusion is built into the workflow, the entire culture transforms from one of subtle resistance to one of shared support and mentorship.

The Implementation System —Solutions and Action Steps

Building a sustainable second-chance program requires transitioning from acknowledging problems to implementing scalable, systemic solutions. This execution phase transforms risk into resilience and intention into reality.

The Five-Step Implementation System: How to Execute

The tactical roadmap for implementation ensures that your program is built on a foundation of honest assessment and proactive support, not guesswork.

1. **Assess and strategize.** The process begins with an honest audit. You must evaluate your organization's current culture, resources, and readiness using anonymous surveys and workshops to identify cultural weak spots. Then, you must identify key roles and processes where second-chance employees can add the most value. Pinpoint high-turnover areas or growth-critical functions where the high loyalty of this talent pool will yield the greatest return on investment.
2. **Build the Framework.** Develop a detailed plan that includes robust onboarding, training, and ongoing support

systems. This plan must formalize mentorship, assigning trained employees to guide new hires, providing a clear safety net and consistent structure. Draft clear policies outlining eligibility, expectations, and support to remove ambiguity and reduce perceived risk for everyone involved. To ensure the project remains manageable, set achievable milestones and celebrate progress to maintain momentum.

3. **Education and Empower.** To combat persistent bias, you must control the narrative. Schedule regular sessions on DEI, including modules specifically tailored to justice-impacted individuals. Crucially, involve HR and legal teams to clarify workplace standards and legal protections. You must educate staff on the benefits and realities of inclusive hiring, using real-world examples and success stories to build belief and replace fear with focused coaching.

4. **Communicate and Validate.** Transparency is key to trust. Announce the program with clear, value-driven messaging, emphasizing safety protocols and professional standards. Regularly update staff and stakeholders on policies, progress, and success stories. Use internal channels to share program metrics (e.g., retention rates) and celebrate the achievements of program participants, shifting the narrative from one of risk to one of competitive advantage.

5. **Monitor and Adjust.** A successful program is a living system that requires constant calibration. Track key performance indicators (KPIs), including retention, promotion rates, and performance ratings. Create channels for open dialogue through anonymous surveys to solicit feedback from all parties. This commitment to monitoring and refining practices ensures the program evolves, addresses friction points quickly, and demonstrates that your commitment is sustained and data driven.

Support Systems: Investing in Retention

Retention is the ultimate metric of success in a second-chance program, and this investment is non-negotiable.

- **Offer Formal Mentorship and Peer Support.** Launch a formalized, budgeted mentorship program where veteran employees are specifically trained to provide professional guidance, not therapy. This is a critical factor in long-term stability.
- **External Resource Partnerships.** Partner with community organizations to offer external support resources like transportation assistance, financial literacy programs, or external counseling. This holistic support demonstrates that the company supports the employee's life stability, not just their job performance, which dramatically lowers recidivism rates and strengthens loyalty.
- **Continuous Feedback.** Implement a formal process for soliciting anonymous feedback from all parties, the new hires, their direct managers, and their co-workers. This commitment builds a learning organization that views every setback as a data point for future improvement.

Case Study: Fresh Start Logistics

Fresh Start Logistics is a mid-sized distribution company facing a critical challenge: chronic talent shortages in their warehouse operations. Turnover rates were high, and recruiting reliable staff was increasingly difficult. The CEO, inspired by the principles outlined in this Chapter 8, decided to look inward for solutions and scale upward by implementing a second-chance employment program.

The CEO recognized that justice-impacted individuals, those with prior convictions seeking a fresh start. represented an untapped talent pool. These candidates often bring a unique perspective, forged by adversity, and demonstrate exceptional motivation and loyalty when given an opportunity.

Leadership Commitment. Fresh Start's leadership began with executive self-reflection. The CEO publicly acknowledged that unconscious bias existed within the company, setting a precedent for transparency and accountability. KPIs for retention and promotion of second-chance hires were tied directly to management performance.

Building the Framework. The company conducted anonymous surveys and workshops to assess readiness. They identified warehouse roles—high-turnover positions where loyalty and reliability were most needed—as ideal for second-chance candidates. A robust onboarding and mentorship program was developed, pairing new hires with trained peer sponsors.

Addressing Concerns. Safety and liability were addressed through standard background checks and leveraging federal bonding programs, which protected the company against financial risk. Town halls were held to educate staff about the program's purpose, emphasizing that inclusion was a strategic solution to talent scarcity, not a risk.

Cultural Integration. Existing employees were invited to participate as mentors and sponsors. Success stories were shared internally, and second-chance employees were encouraged (voluntarily) to speak about their journeys. This direct exposure helped dissolve stereotypes and fostered a culture of support.

Continuous Improvement. KPIs such as retention, promotion rates, and performance were tracked. Anonymous feedback channels allowed all employees to voice concerns and suggestions, ensuring the program evolved and friction points were addressed quickly.

The Results. Within a year, Fresh Start Logistics saw a dramatic reduction in turnover and a measurable increase in productivity. Second-chance employees demonstrated higher engagement and loyalty, and the company's reputation for social responsibility attracted new customers and partners. The inclusive culture boosted morale across all teams, transforming the workplace into a source of pride and resilience.

Summary: The Strategic Imperative of Second-Chance Inclusion

The question is no longer *if* your business should implement second-chance employment, but why you must fully commit to overcoming internal bias to make it work. The motivation transcends mere ethics; it is a fundamental strategic imperative, delivering a powerful collection of long-term business advantages.

Business Growth: Unlocking a Hidden Talent Pipeline

The first and most immediate dividend is growing your business by opening a hidden talent pipeline. Overcoming internal biases and implementing a structured program grants you access to a loyal, motivated, and productive workforce that your competitors are overlooking. This talent pool provides a reliable labor source that directly fuels growth and serves as a crucial defense against the crippling cost of talent scarcity that plagues most industries. By focusing on potential over past mistakes, you gain a dedicated workforce that sees employment as a cornerstone of stability.

Culture Transformation: The Engine of Retention

This commitment transforms your internal climate, creating a ripple effect known as culture transformation. This is the engine of retention. A truly inclusive environment dramatically boosts morale, retention, and innovation across all teams. When a company walks the talk by actively investing in human potential, the entire culture is lifted with a sense of purpose. Existing employees naturally rise to become mentors, coaches, and leaders, finding a deeper professional meaning in their daily work, which ultimately strengthens organizational bonds and resilience.

Reputation & Responsibility: Walking the Talk

Externally, this initiative secures your standing in the modern marketplace, upping your reputation as a responsible leader by walking the talk. By running a successful, transparent program, your company secures a powerful reputational advantage. This commitment distinguishes your brand and attracts socially conscious customers, investors, and vendors, solidifying your ethical leadership. This responsible hiring practice aligns your social impact with your business goals, proving that doing good is good business.

Competitive Advantage: A Defensible Moat

This combined internal and external strength creates a significant barrier to entry for your rivals, establishing a competitive advantage, akin to a defensible moat. Most competitors won't make the investment required to dismantle their old biases and implement these systematic changes. They will remain shackled by their traditional recruiting methods, leaving you with an enduring competitive moat and a workforce that is often more stable and motivated than the market average.

Sustainable Success: Inclusion as Resilience

Ultimately, the commitment to second-chance employment is an investment in sustainable success once you understand inclusion as resilience. It proves that your company can adapt, learn, and grow by focusing on potential over history. This inherent ability to look inward, challenge cultural assumptions, and access non-traditional resources is the hallmark of a business built for sustainable, exponential success. The program demonstrates organizational maturity and capacity for positive change, proving that the answer to your talent needs truly is in the building.

EPILOGUE: THE ARCHITECT WITHIN

The Building, The Blueprint and a New Vision

The **Answers Are in the Building.** This was the singular, powerful premise that launched our shared journey—and it is the enduring truth we must carry forward.

We began this book recognizing a common failure: the relentless tendency for organizations to look for silver-bullet answers, as well as to the distant horizon, all while overlooking the most valuable knowledge right at their feet.

The building is not just brick and mortar. It is the living, breathing system of your organization—the culture, the communication pathways, the habits of inquiry, and the collective, unmined wisdom held within your own walls.

This book is, therefore, a field guide for a fundamental shift in perception where a leader no longer views themselves as a mere manager. Instead, they embrace the role of the **Chief Architect of Learning**. We sought to teach you how to read the blueprint of your own company, recognizing that every error, every success, and every casual conversation is a line drawn on the master plan. The problems we struggled with, we realized, were simply reflections of the systems we built to solve them.

The Discipline of Deep Listening

As we close this final chapter, we recognize that the principles explored across Chapters 1 through 8 are not complex frameworks. They are acts of personal leadership discipline. They challenge the conventional notion of power that the highest office must possess the greatest knowledge.

Instead, your new mandate is to embody the humility necessary to accept that the deepest knowledge resides at the periphery, held by the people closest to the customer, the process, and the pain.

Think of the lessons of inquiry-driven communication (Chapter 3) and the systemic discipline of closing the knowledge loop (Chapter 6). These are not corporate mandates. They are personal commitments that require you to create a space where you speak less and listen more. This is the act of deep listening, where you actively seek data that might contradict your own assumptions.

The organization is a vast, continuous schoolhouse. Your job is to be the steward of psychological safety, and to design the systems and spaces that make it easy for truth to travel uphill, quickly and cleanly.

The answers are in the building, yes, but only if you, the leader, have intentionally designed the plumbing and wiring of the organization to carry the signal of truth to your desk.

Your Personal Blueprint for Action

This is where inspiration must become intention. As you leave these pages, carry with you a redefined sense of what it means to lead:

EPILOGUE: THE ARCHITECT WITHIN

- **Embrace Humility as a Tool, not a Virtue.** Your goal is not to appear humble, but to use humility as the most powerful data-gathering tool available. Go to the source (Chapter 2), ask the naive question, and study the errors (Chapter 4) as if they were treasure maps leading to innovation.
- **Architect Psychological Safety.** Recognize that fear is the ultimate suppressor of truth (Chapter 7). Your most important design decision is creating a cultural foundation where an employee is rewarded for raising a problem, not punished for exposing a flaw. Your commitment to radical transparency must start with your own radical vulnerability.
- **Lead with Inquiry.** Stop leading with fixed solutions. Start leading with open, simple questions that force collaborative discovery (Chapter 1). "What did we learn today? What surprised you? What would we regret not changing?" These are the levers that move entire organizations, and they are wielded by the leader who can genuinely suspend judgment.

The Construction of the Future

The most successful leaders are not those who leave behind a grand, finished plan, but those who leave behind a culture capable of perpetual self-correction and limitless growth.

The "building" you inhabit is merely a manifestation of the collective answers you possess right now. The building of tomorrow, the one that will thrive amidst continuous change, must be built on better, faster, and more honest answers.

This is your final, personal moment of accountability. The knowledge has been illuminated. The principles for a more dynamic, honest, and intelligent organization are now etched into your mindset.

The journey ahead demands that you transition from the reader of this book to the **Architect of Inquiry** within your own world.

Go forth, listen deeply, and build the future by honoring the institutional genius that resides within your building.

We thank you for taking the time to read our book and for the commitment you are making to consider and implement these ideas for your organization.

Jeff Baldassari & Leslie Morales

ABOUT THE AUTHORS

Jeff Baldassari is the Founder & CEO of The Competitive Edge Group, a fractional CEO consultancy based in Newport Beach, CA, dedicated to solving complex scaling problems for business leaders and owners.

Jeff possesses 21 years of CEO experience, where he successfully mastered the process needed to transform and rapidly scale businesses. He has also served on seven corporate and organizational boards.

Jeff provide business leaders with a proven methodology to overcome challenges. This practical process is focused on two key drivers: building durable operating systems and unlocking team engagement to drive exponential, sustainable growth.

Leslie Morales, COO of The Competitive Edge Group, equips business leaders and CEOs with a proven framework to navigate complex challenges. Its practical approach centers on two critical success factors: establishing resilient operational systems and fostering deep team engagement to fuel scalable growth.

With three decades of executive leadership—including a distinguished career at Enterprise Rent-A-Car and VP roles across multiple industries, Leslie brings award-winning performance and strategic expertise to every engagement.

She is a recognized leader in Second Chance Employment, having successfully integrated justice-involved individuals into the workforce through partnerships with nonprofits and workforce development agencies.